Two Sure Ways

to

INCREASE

Your

FAITH

(Dynamic Factors of Faith)

Available at
www.BurningHeartBibleStudies.com
(and most booksellers)

Two Sure Ways

to

INCREASE

Your

FAITH

(Dynamic Factors of Faith)

Chuck Bagby, PhD

BURNING HEART BIBLE STUDIES™

San Antonio, Texas, USA

Available at
www.BurningHeartBibleStudies.com
(and most booksellers)

Published in San Antonio, Texas by Burning Heart Bible Studies (www.BurningHeartBibleStudies.com). Burning Heart Bible Studies, the Burning Heart Bible Studies logo, Bagby Translation, and BT are trademarks of Burning Heart Bible Studies.

BT (Bagby Translation) designates a passage of Scripture translated by Dr. Chuck Bagby.

Scripture quotations marked NASU (New American Standard Bible Update) cite the New American Standard Bible® 1995 updated translation, New American Standard Bible® Copyright© 1960, 1962, 1963, 1968, 1971, 1972, 1973, 1975, 1977, 1995 by The Lockman Foundation (www.Lockman.org). Used by permission.

ISBN (International Standard Book Number) 978-0-9911520-3-2

LCCN (Library of Congress Control Number) 2017918074

To the grandchildren of Chuck and Robin Bagby,
May you forever use your talents to further Jesus' kingdom.

Kayley

Charlie

Demos

Zach

Layla

Aravis

C.J.

Hana

Corbin

Samantha

Owen

Acknowledgements

I thank members of the Christian Writers Group of Greater San Antonio who skillfully critiqued the manuscript of *Two Sure Ways to Increase Your Faith*: Brenda Blanchard, Richard Barnett, Brian Veneklase, Phillip Williams, Jonathan Hardy, Mint Newman, and Rudy Dumapias. I also extend gratitude to the book's Beta readers for helping to ensure the high quality of the manuscript: Pam Connell, John Lange, Eden Stewart Martin, Eric Martin, Sandy Martin, Paul McQuien, and Carol Otremba.

Without the enduring patience and devoted support of my wife, I would have found it impossible to pursue writing. Robin, I love and appreciate you dearly.

Any glory drawn by this work I direct toward God, who by His grace prepared me to undertake the task at hand.

Contents

Preface

Do you desire to increase your faith in God and guarantee its continued growth? Within the following pages you will learn the simple fundamentals of faith and discover two sure ways to strengthen *your* faith.

Had I understood faith better earlier in my life, I would have had greater productivity as God's servant. Since I cannot return to the past to begin my journey anew, I will share what I wish I had known as I optimistically spur *your* faith forward.

Meanwhile, bear in mind the apostle Paul's counsel to the Christians in Rome,

> *The faith which you have,*
> *have as your own conviction before God.*[1]

---

[1] Romans 14:22 NASU (New American Standard Bible Update, 1995 revision). For more information about the NASU, see the copyright page, among the first pages of this book.

....

CHAPTER 1

Faith in Action

Abraham's Sacrifice of His Son

Abraham[2] grew up prior to 2003 B.C.[3] in Ur,[4] a harbor city lying on the northern coast of the Persian Gulf.[5] God motivated Abraham to abandon his home, telling him,

> *Go forth from your country, and from your relatives and from your father's house, to the land which I will show you; and I will make you a great nation.*[6]

His final destiny, Canaan, lay several hundred miles west of Ur, near the Mediterranean Sea.

---

[2] Originally called Abram, God later changed Abram's name to Abraham (Genesis 17:5).

[3] Abraham most likely departed Ur before 2003 B.C., the year the Elamites conquered and destroyed the city.

[4] Genesis 11:27-29

[5] Over the ages, the coastline withdrew southeastward, placing the ruins of Ur about 150 miles (240 kilometers) northwest of the Persian Gulf and six miles (10 kilometers) south of the Euphrates River.

[6] Genesis 12:1-2 NASU; Acts 7:2-4

Map: Ur

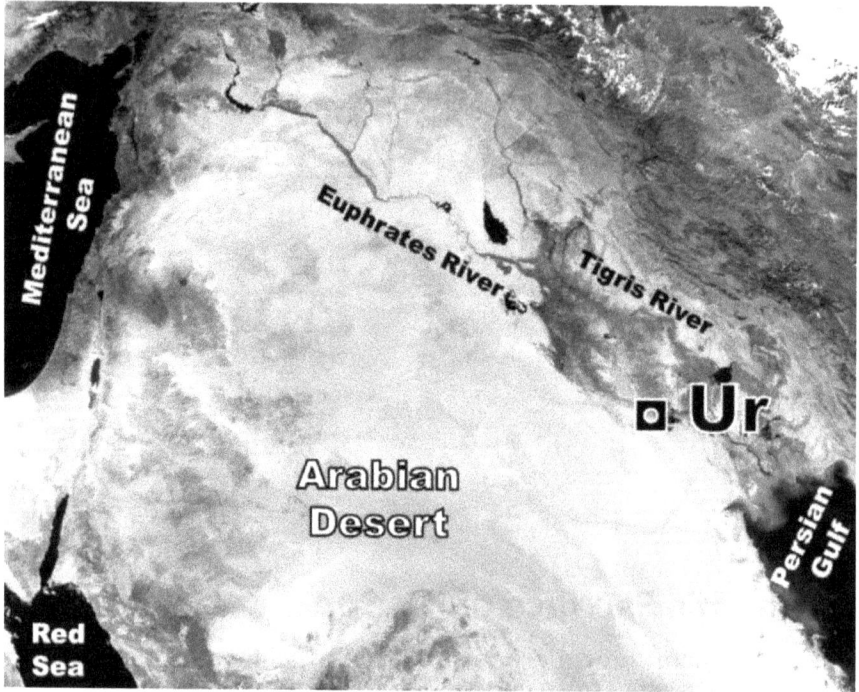

Figure 1 - 1

Ziggurat of Ur (Temple of the Moon Goddess Nanna, 1932 A.D.)

Figure 1 - 2

Ruins of Ur (Looking from Top of Ziggurat, 1932 A.D.)

Figure 1 - 3

Ruins of Ur (1932 A.D.)

Figure 1 - 4

Ruins of Ur (Courtyard and Houses, 1932 A.D.)

Figure 1 - 5

Abraham's Route from Ur to Haran to Canaan

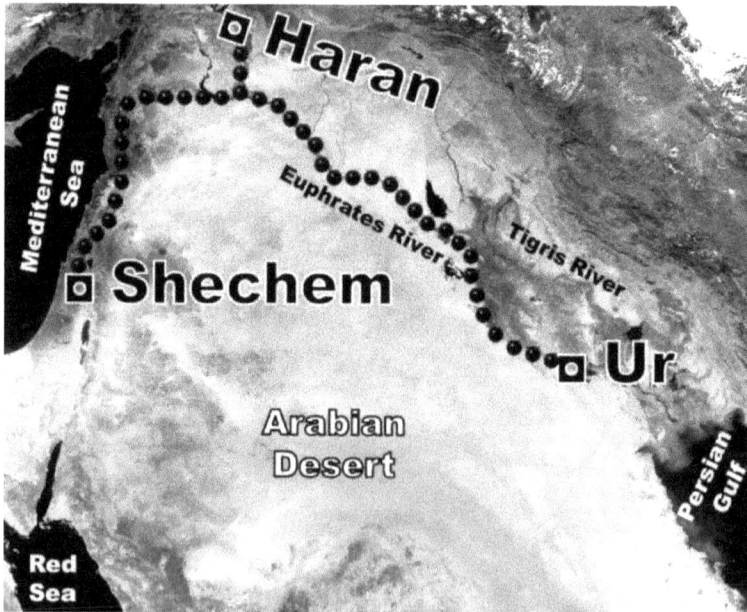

Figure 1 - 6

Following Abraham's arrival in Canaan, God challenged his faith, instructing him to sacrifice his son, Isaac.[7] Raising a knife over the altar to slay Isaac, Abraham's hands likely trembled as tears drained off his beard. Even so, Abraham maintained confidence in God's pledge to develop his descendants into "a great nation."[8] He reasoned that God possessed the power to bring Isaac back to life in order to fulfill His promise.[9] Before the knife slit Isaac's throat, God sent an angel to stop Abraham from completing the sacrifice.[10]

Due to Abraham's trusting works of faith, God declared him righteous,[11] and "he was called a friend of God."[12] Carrying through His commitment to make Abraham "a great nation,"[13] God indeed ensured that Isaac's descendants flourished. The descendants of Jacob (Isaac's son, Abraham's grandson) became the nation of Israel.[14]

***

The Story from God's Scriptures

Now it came about ..., that God tested Abraham, and said to him, ... "Take now your son, ... Isaac, ... and offer him ... as a burnt offering on one of the mountains of which I will tell you."

So Abraham rose early in the morning and saddled his donkey, and took two of his young men with him and Isaac his son; and he split wood for the burnt offering, ... and went to the place of which God had told him. On the third day

---

[7] Genesis 22:1-18
[8] Genesis 12:2 NASU
[9] Hebrews 11:17-19
[10] Genesis 22:10-12
[11] James 2:21-24; A few other Scriptures that discuss Abraham's faith include Genesis 11:26-12:6, Genesis 22:1-18, Acts 7:2-4, and Hebrews 11:17-19.
[12] James 2:23 BT
[13] Genesis 12:2 NASU
[14] Romans 11:1; 2 Corinthians 11:22

Abraham raised his eyes and saw the place from a distance.

Abraham said to his young men, "Stay here with the donkey, and I and the lad will go over there; and we will worship and return to you."

Abraham took the wood of the burnt offering and laid it on Isaac his son, and he took in his hand the fire and the knife. So the two of them walked on together.

Isaac spoke to Abraham ..., "Behold, the fire and the wood, but where is the lamb for the burnt offering?"

Abraham said, "God will provide for Himself the lamb for the burnt offering, my son."

So the two of them walked on together. Then they came to the place of which God had told him; and Abraham built the altar there and arranged the wood, and bound his son Isaac and laid him on the altar, on top of the wood. Abraham ... took the knife to slay his son.

But the angel of the Lord called to him from heaven and said, ... "Do not stretch out your hand against the lad, and do nothing to him; for ... you fear God, since you have not withheld your son ... from Me."

Then Abraham raised his eyes and looked, and behold, behind him a ram caught in the thicket by his horns; and Abraham ... took the ram and offered him up for a burnt offering in the place of his son.[15]

---

[15] Genesis 22:1-13 NASU (New American Standard Update, 1995 revision)

Shadrach, Meshach, & Abed-nego

In 597 B.C., King Nebuchadnezzar[16] of Babylonia conquered the Kingdom of Judah. Daniel, along with his friends, Shadrach, Meshach, and Abed-nego, found themselves among the tens of thousands who became reluctant Judahite colonists in foreign lands as the Babylonians relocated them to various regions of the Babylonian Empire. Regardless, Daniel thrived within his new environment, together with his companions.

***

The Story from God's Scriptures

Then the king promoted Daniel and ... made him ruler over the whole province of Babylon and chief prefect over all the wise men of Babylon.

And Daniel made request of the king, and he appointed Shadrach, Meshach and Abed-nego over the administration of the province of Babylon, while Daniel was at the king's court.

Nebuchadnezzar the king made an image of gold, the height of which was sixty cubits[17] and its width six cubits;[18] ... Then ... the king sent word to assemble ... all the rulers of the provinces to come to the dedication of the image ...

The herald loudly proclaimed: "To you the command is given, O peoples, nations and men of every language, that at the moment you hear the sound of the horn, flute, lyre, trigon, psaltery and bagpipe and all kinds of music, you are to fall down and worship the golden image ... But whoever does not fall down and worship shall immediately be cast into the midst of a furnace of blazing fire." ...

---

[16] Nebuchadnezzar (nĕb-ü-khăd-nĕz-zər)
[17] 90 feet (27.4 meters)
[18] 9 feet (2.7 meters)

When all the peoples heard ... all kinds of music, ... [they][19] *fell down and worshiped the golden image ... For this reason ... certain Chaldeans came forward and brought charges against the Jews.*

They ... said to Nebuchadnezzar ... "O king, live forever! You, O king, have made a decree that every man ... is to fall down and worship the golden image. But whoever does not fall down and worship shall be cast into the midst of a furnace of blazing fire. There are certain Jews whom you have appointed over the administration of the province of Babylon, namely Shadrach, Meshach and Abed-nego. These men, ... do not ... worship the golden image ..."

Then Nebuchadnezzar in rage ... gave orders to bring Shadrach, Meshach and Abed-nego ...

Nebuchadnezzar ... said to them, "Is it true, ... that you do not serve my gods or worship the golden image that I have set up? Now if you are ready ... to fall down and worship the image that I have made, very well. But if you do not worship, you will immediately be cast into the midst of a furnace of blazing fire; and what god is there who can deliver you out of my hands?"

Shadrach, Meshach and Abed-nego replied to the king, "O Nebuchadnezzar, we do not need to give you an answer concerning this matter. If it be so, our God whom we serve is able to deliver us from the furnace of blazing fire; and He will deliver us out of your hand, O king. But even if He does not, let it be known to you, O king, that we are not going to serve your gods or worship the golden image that you have set up."

Then Nebuchadnezzar was filled with wrath ... He answered by giving orders to heat the furnace seven times more than it was usually heated. ... Then these men were tied

---

[19] The author added [they] to provide grammatical consistency.

up ... and were cast into the midst of the furnace of blazing fire. ...

Then ... the king was astounded and stood up in haste; he said to his high officials, "Was it not three men we cast bound into the midst of the fire?"

They replied to the king, "Certainly, O king."

He said, "Look! I see four men loosed and walking about in the midst of the fire without harm, and the appearance of the fourth is like a son of the gods!"

Then Nebuchadnezzar came near to the door of the furnace ... and said, "... come out, you servants of the Most High God, and come here!"

Then Shadrach, Meshach and Abed-nego came out of the midst of the fire. The ... king's high officials gathered around and saw ... that the fire had no effect on the bodies of these men nor was the hair of their head singed, nor were their trousers damaged, nor had the smell of fire even come upon them.

Nebuchadnezzar ... said, "Blessed be the God of Shadrach, Meshach and Abed-nego, who has sent His angel and delivered His servants who put their trust in Him, violating the king's command, and yielded up their bodies so as not to serve or worship any god except their own God. ..."

Then the king caused Shadrach, Meshach and Abed-nego to prosper in the province of Babylon.[20]

---

[20] Daniel 2:48-3:30 NASU

Daniel in the Lion's Den

In 550 B.C., Cyrus the Great began to establish the Persian Empire, sometimes referred to by historians as the Medo-Persian Empire.[21] Intent on building the world's preeminent kingdom, he pushed his army southward toward the Babylonian Empire. On October 12, 539 B.C., he launched a surprise attack on Babylon.[22] Seventeen days later, Cyrus the Great entered the city victoriously.

Shortly thereafter, Cyrus delegated the rule of Babylonia to Darius,[23] one of his generals. Josephus[24] mentioned Darius had family ties with Cyrus the Great. (Josephus, 1977, p. 226)[25] He governed Babylonia on behalf of Cyrus the Great from 539-525 B.C.

Cyrus also allowed the Judeans (Judahites) in Babylonian territories to return to their homeland, his policy concerning ethnic groups displaced by previous conquerors. Even so, Daniel and most of the families deported from the Kingdom of Judah by Nebuchadnezzar chose to remain in Babylonian regions.

According to Josephus, Darius selected three "presidents" to govern his 360 districts within Babylonia. (Josephus, 1977, p. 226)[26] In Daniel's written record of those times, he referred to the presidents as *commissioners* who presided over Babylonia.[27] Eventually, Darius gave Daniel responsibility over all Babylonia.[28]

---

21 Medo-Persian Empire – short for Median-Persian Empire

22 Babylon – capital city of Babylonia

23 Historians also refer to Darius by the names Gubaru, Ugbaru, and Gobryas. In his historical account, Daniel refers to him by the name Darius six times (Daniel 6:1,6,9,25,28; 9:1) and twice as "Darius the Mede" (Daniel 5:31; 11:1).

24 Titus Flavius Josephus (jō-sḗ-fəs), a Jewish general and historian, lived 37-100 A.D. For more information regarding Josephus, see "Glossary."

25 The Antiquities of the Jews, Book 10, Chapter 11, Paragraph 4

26 The Antiquities of the Jews, Book 10, Chapter 11, Paragraph 4

27 Daniel 6:1-3

28 Daniel 6:3,28

Josephus commented that Darius held "Daniel in very great esteem, and made him the principal of his friends." (Josephus, 1977, p. 227)[29]

***

The Story from God's Scriptures

It seemed good to Darius to appoint 120 satraps[30] over the kingdom,[31] that they would be in charge of the whole kingdom, and over them three commissioners (of whom Daniel was one), that these satraps might be accountable to them, and that the king might not suffer loss. Then this Daniel began distinguishing himself among the commissioners and satraps because he possessed an extraordinary spirit, and the king planned to appoint him over the entire kingdom.

Then the commissioners and satraps began trying to find a ground of accusation against Daniel in regard to government affairs; but they could find no ground of accusation or evidence of corruption ...

These men said, "We will not find any ground of accusation against this Daniel unless we find it against him with regard to the law of his God."

Then these commissioners and satraps came by agreement to the king and spoke to him as follows: "King Darius, live forever! All the commissioners of the kingdom, the prefects and the satraps, the high officials and the governors have consulted together that the king should establish a statute and enforce an injunction that anyone who makes a petition to any god or man besides you, O king, for thirty days, shall be cast into the lions' den. Now, O king, establish the injunction and sign the document so that it may

---

[29] *The Antiquities of the Jews*, Book 10, Chapter 11, Paragraph 7

[30] Satrap (săˊ-trăp) – governor of a provincial district within the Persian Empire

[31] Kingdom = Babylonia, recently conquered by Cyrus the Great and incorporated into the Persian Empire.

not be changed, according to the law of the Medes and Persians, which may not be revoked."

Therefore King Darius signed ... the injunction.

Now when Daniel knew that the document was signed, he entered his house (now in his roof chamber he had windows open toward Jerusalem); and he continued kneeling on his knees three times a day, praying and giving thanks before his God, as he had been doing previously. Then these men ... found Daniel making petition and supplication before his God. ...

They approached ... the king ..., "Did you not sign an injunction that any man who makes a petition to any god or man besides you, O king, for thirty days, is to be cast into the lions' den?"

The king replied, "The statement is true, according to the law of the Medes and Persians, which may not be revoked."

Then they answered ..., "Daniel, who is one of the exiles from Judah, pays no attention to you, O king, or to the injunction which you signed, but keeps making his petition three times a day."

Then, as soon as the king heard this statement, he was deeply distressed and set his mind on delivering Daniel; and even until sunset he kept exerting himself to rescue him.

Then these men ... said to the king, "Recognize, O king, that it is a law of the Medes and Persians that no injunction or statute which the king establishes may be changed."

Then the king gave orders, and Daniel was ... cast into the lions' den. The king ... said to Daniel, "Your God whom you constantly serve will Himself deliver you."

A stone was ... laid over the mouth of the den; and the king sealed it with his own signet ring and with the signet rings of his nobles, so that nothing would be changed in regard to Daniel.

Then the king went off to his palace and spent the night fasting, and no entertainment was brought before him; and his sleep fled from him. Then the king arose at dawn ... and went in haste to the lions' den.

When he had come near the den ..., he cried out with a troubled voice ..., "Daniel, servant of the living God, has your God, whom you constantly serve, been able to deliver you from the lions?"

Then Daniel spoke to the king, "O king, live forever! My God sent His angel and shut the lions' mouths and they have not harmed me, inasmuch as I was found innocent before Him; and also toward you, O king, I have committed no crime."

Then the king was very pleased and gave orders for Daniel to be taken up out of the den ... and no injury whatever was found on him, because he had trusted in his God. ...

Then Darius ... wrote to all the peoples, nations and men of every language who were living in all the land: "May your peace abound! I make a decree that in all the dominion of my kingdom men are to fear and tremble before the God of Daniel; For He is the living God and enduring forever ..."

So this Daniel enjoyed success in the reign of Darius and in the reign of Cyrus the Persian.[32]

---

[32] Daniel 6:1-28 NASU

CHAPTER 2

....

Help!

How?

How!

Sacrifice your son to God?

Choose a blazing furnace rather than bow to a big piece of gold?

Prefer to face hungry lions sooner than stop talking to God for 30 days?

How could Abraham, Shadrach, Meshach, Abed-nego, and Daniel have had such strong faith? Can you and I gain that level of faith? How can we overcome our faithlessness? The father of a demon-possessed boy expressed the same concern to Jesus.

Help My Faithlessness!

After giving sight to a blind man on the northern coast of the Sea of Galilee,[33] Jesus led His twelve friends about 24 miles[34] northward through a lush plain to the villages around the city of Caesarea Philippi.[35]

Upon descending from a prayer excursion[36] on a nearby mountain with Peter, James, and John, Jesus discovered a group of Jewish scribes[37] arguing with His other nine apostles.[38]

Recognizing Jesus, the crowd rushed to greet Him.

***

The Story from God's Scriptures

And He asked them, "What are you discussing with them?"[39]

And one of the crowd answered Him, "Teacher, I brought You my son, possessed with a spirit which makes him mute; and whenever it seizes him, it slams him to the ground

---

[33] Mark 8:22-26

[34] 39 kilometers

[35] Mark 8:27

[36] Luke 9:28,37

[37] Scribes – also referred to as *lawyers,* in relation to the Law of Moses and the religious traditions of the Jewish elders (Matthew 22:35; Luke 7:30; 10:25; 11:45-46,52; 14:3); For more information concerning scribes, see "Glossary."

[38] Apostle – *transliteration* of the Greek word *apóstolos* (ä-pǒ-stǒ-lǒs), ἀπόστολος, a common Greek word describing any delegate. When *transliterating*, a translator spells out an approximation of the original language's pronunciation of a word, using the alphabet of the second language. Within the Scriptures, "apostles" typically refers to the 12 followers chosen by Jesus to officially represent Him. For lists of the original twelve, see Matthew 10:1-4; Mark 3:13-19; Luke 6:12-16; and Acts 1:13 (which excludes Judas Iscariot, who had died).

[39] Mark 9:16 NASU

and he foams at the mouth, and grinds his teeth and stiffens out.[40] *...*

They brought the boy to Him. When he saw Him, immediately the spirit threw him into a convulsion, and falling to the ground, he began rolling around and foaming at the mouth.[41]

And He asked his father, "How long has this been happening to him?"

And he said, "From childhood. It has often thrown him both into the fire and into the water to destroy him. But if You can do anything, take pity on us and help us!"[42]

Then Jesus said to him, "If You can? Everything is possible for the one who has faith."[43]

*Immediately the young child's father shouted out, saying, "I have faith; **help my faithlessness**!"*[44]

Then, Jesus denounced the demon and it came out of the boy, and he was restored to health that moment.[45]

***

This unfortunate father told Jesus, "I have faith." His faith had led him to bring his son to Jesus. Nevertheless, he feared the insufficiency of his faith may prevent the healing of his son. In desperation, he cried out to Jesus, "Help my faithlessness!"

---

[40] Mark 9.17-18 NASU

[41] Mark 9:20 NASU

[42] Mark 9:21-22 NASU

[43] Mark 9:23 BT – BT (Bagby Translation) designates a passage of Scripture translated by Dr. Chuck Bagby. For more information regarding the BT, see "Appendix 6: Baghy Translation (BT)."

[44] Mark 9:24 BT; For emphasis, the author has placed selected words in bold font within passages of Scripture quoted in this book. Although the bold highlights do not exist in the original language text, they help the reader follow the logical thought of passages.

[45] Matthew 17:18 BT

***

<u>*Contemplation Points*</u>

1. Do you empathize with the father?

    a. If so, why?

    b. If not, why not?

2. Do you question the adequacy of your faith?

    a. If so, why?

    b. If not, why not?

Increase Our Faith!

Around three years later, Jesus passed through a village about a three-day walk north of Jerusalem.[46] He taught tough lessons regarding godly conduct to the horde of followers who trailed Him.[47]

> *Be on your guard! If your brother sins, rebuke him; and if he repents, forgive him. And if he sins against you seven times a day, and returns to you seven times, saying, "I repent," forgive him.*
>
> *The apostles said to the Lord, "**Increase our faith!**"*[48]

As with other lessons Jesus taught, Peter found this one difficult to grasp. Unsure of his understanding, he sought clarification.

> *Then Peter came and said to Him, "Lord, how often shall my brother sin against me and I forgive him? Up to seven times?"*
>
> *Jesus said to him, "I do not say to **you**, up to seven times, but up to seventy times seven."*[49]

Jesus explained His expectation. Regardless, His apostles felt overwhelmed by the challenge. No wonder they pled with Him, "Increase our faith!"[50] Don't feel alone if you have done the same. I have, too.

A little reflection reveals that the answer to our request for stronger faith rests within us, by God's design. In the following pages, you will discover God's plan for enhancing your faith.

---

[46] Luke 13:22,31-33
[47] Luke 14:25-35
[48] Luke 17:3-5 NASU
[49] Matthew 18:21-22 NASU
[50] Luke 17:5 NASU

***

Contemplation Points

1. Do you possess faith in God?

   a. If so, how do you know?

   b. If not, why not?

2. Write *your* definition of faith in one sentence.

CHAPTER 3

....

Faith Defined by God

Where is your faith?
(Jesus to His apostles)[51]

    With a multitude of people trailing Him, Jesus walked to a hillside overlooking the Sea of Galilee. After He sat down, the followers gathered, and He began to correct some of the false traditional religious teachings their culture embraced.

    Five times Jesus explained,

    "You have heard that it was said ... But I tell you ...."[52]

He would have to do the same today concerning the topic of faith. He would remind us of what we have heard, and then reveal the true nature of the faith God would have us maintain.

---

[51] Luke 8:25 NASU
[52] Matthew 5:21-22,27-28,33-34,38-39,43-44 NASU

Our culture typically portrays faith as *subjective*, an emotional experience that eludes logic and rational evidence, a *feeling* of trust. Beware! Don't accept the world's definitions of God's words. Don't rely on fallible human opinions to understand the faith God intends you to attain. Don't depend on trendy religious theologies[53] to understand God's mind-set concerning faith. Instead, discover His definition by noting how *He* used the term *faith* in His Scriptures.

In the 11th chapter of Hebrews, God explained the nature of the faith He desires us to possess.[54] In contrast to the subjective, sensationalistic perspective many human theologies resonate, God described faith as necessarily *objective*,[55] requiring a factual foundation.

*Faith is the **substantiation**[56] of things being hoped for,*
*the **conviction**[57] of things not seen.*
(Hebrews 11:1 BT)

---

[53] Theology, when referred to in this work, consists of any human-crafted system of religious interpretations, traditions, creeds, opinions, legends, myths, or combination of these items compiled or promoted by a religious leader, sect, denomination, or organization.

[54] God, through one of His prophets, provided His definition of faith in Hebrews 11:1. All Scripture written by God's prophets serves as a message from God, as explained by the apostle Paul to the evangelist Timothy in 2 Timothy 3:16-17. For a few additional passages that indicate God spoke through His prophets, see 2 Samuel 23:2; Luke 1:70; Acts 1:16; Acts 3:18; Acts 28:25; 2 Peter 1:20-21.

[55] Objective – based on logic rather than feelings

[56] A discussion of *substantiation* occurs a couple of pages forward.

[57] A discussion of *conviction* occurs several pages forward.

A grammatical tool called *synthetic parallelism*[58] takes place in Hebrews 11:1. When synthetic parallelism appears in language, a subsequent thought expands on the concept expressed in the first thought. In Hebrews 11:1, the second phrase, "the *conviction* of things not seen," builds on the meaning of the first phrase, "the *substantiation* of things being hoped for."

Although "of things being hoped for" and "of things unseen" both refer to the heavenly realm awaiting faithful Christians, the nouns *substantiation* and *conviction* differ in meaning. They do not serve as synonyms,[59] but rather complement one another. Neither "the *substantiation* of things hoped for" nor "the *conviction* of things unseen" defines faith on its own. Each requires the other to formulate the faith God detailed throughout Hebrews chapter 11.

Remain receptive to God's perspective concerning faith, as we continue to examine the meanings of the words and phrases used within His definition.

*Faith is the **substantiation**[60] of things being hoped for,*
*the **conviction**[61] of things not seen.*
(Hebrews 11:1 BT)

---

[58] Parallelism –For information regarding parallelism and its different types, see "Glossary."

[59] Synonymous words have the same meaning or nearly the same meaning.

[60] A discussion of *substantiation* occurs a couple of pages forward.

[61] A discussion of *conviction* occurs several pages forward.

Faith (Pístis)

Although the Greek[62] word *pístis* (pĭs-tĭs)[63] often translates as "faith," the context[64] in which a biblical writer used the word dictates whether a translator should render it "belief," "trust," or "faith." The word "faith" best matches most uses of *pístis* and its various grammatical forms throughout Hebrews chapter 11.

According to God's definition, faith consists of two essential factors: *substantiation* and *conviction*. The absence of either fundamental fails to complete the faith God expects of us. Our correct understanding and acceptance of *His* definition of faith proves crucial, for "without faith, it is impossible to please Him."[65]

Substantiation (*Hupóstasis*)

Hupóstasis (hüp-ŏ-stä-sĭs),[66] an early-Greek technical and scientific term, here translated "substantiation,"[67] forms a compound noun. The first part of the word, *hupó* (hüp-ŏ),[68] means "**sub-**, under."

---

[62] The authors of the New Testament books and correspondence wrote their works in Greek. Greek served as an international language during the first century A.D. due to the enduring Hellenistic (Greek) influence of Alexander the Great's vast conquests three centuries earlier, as he expanded his Macedonian Empire. By writing in Greek, New Testament authors effectively communicated within the Roman Empire, as well as non-Roman Mediterranean cultures.

[63] *Pístis* (pĭs-tĭs), πίστις, nominative singular feminine noun

[64] Context, the communication before and after a word or passage, often sheds light on the meaning intended by the writer or speaker.

[65] Hebrews 11:6 NASU

[66] *Hupóstasis* (hŭ-pŏs-tä-sĭs), ὑπόστασις, nominative singular feminine noun

[67] In lieu of the word "substantiation," some translators have utilized terms such as "substance," "assurance," "reality," "title deed," "confidence," and "certainty." Although those words serve as suitable translations of *hupóstasis* within other contexts, none of them effectively clarifies God's definition of faith in the context of Hebrews chapter 11 as His prophet intended in the Greek text.

[68] *Hupó* (hŭ-pŏ), ὑπό

The second part of the noun, *stásis* (stắ-sĭs),[69] denotes "-**stantiation**, standing." God explained that faith requires *hupóstasis* (substantiation),[70] validation based on the examination of credible evidence. Once substantiated, an issue becomes a matter of fact (i.e., knowledge).

The faith God intends His people to possess cannot exist without substantiation (knowledge). For this reason, He guided His prophets throughout antiquity to write precisely the history we need to substantiate our faith. For example, He led Matthew, Mark, Luke, and John to record facts of Jesus' life and teachings, the facts we use to substantiate our faith in Him.

Hours from betrayal by Judas, Jesus prayed to the Father concerning you and me. He described *us* as those who will substantiate their faith by considering the words of His apostles. He implored the Father, saying,

> *"I do not ask on behalf of these* [the apostles][71] *alone, but for* **those also who believe in Me through their word**; *that they may all be one; even as You, Father, are in Me and I in You, that they also may be in Us, so that the world may believe that You sent Me."*[72]

John, a beloved friend of Jesus, explained toward the conclusion of his biography of Jesus that he intended his readers to substantiate their faith through his writings. He stated,

> *Many other signs Jesus also performed in the presence of the disciples, which are not written in this book; but* **these have been written so that you may believe** ....[73]

---

[69] *Stásis* (stắ-sĭs), στάσις
[70] Substantiation = sub (under) + stantiation (standing)
[71] The author added [the apostles] to clarify the context.
[72] John 17:20-21 NASU
[73] John 20:30-31 NASU

John later spoke on behalf of all the prophets who walked with Jesus on Earth, providing substantiation for our faith by writing,

> *What was from the beginning,*[74] *what we have **heard**, what we have **seen** with our eyes, what we have looked at and **touched** with our hands, concerning the Word of Life*[75] *– and the life was manifested, and we have **seen** and **testify** and **proclaim** to you the eternal life,*[76] *which was with the Father and was manifested to us – what we have **seen** and **heard** we **proclaim** to you also, so that you too may have fellowship with us ....*[77]

God selected only some of His prophets to write His Scriptures.[78] For ages, He safeguarded copies of those Scriptures for us, so we would have means by which to substantiate our faith in Him. He preserved and delivered the facts – substantiation.

Upon recognizing the importance of substantiation to faith, the rationale of the Hebrew writer's statement, "by faith we understand,"[79] becomes apparent. Faith demands knowledge, facts substantiated by credible evidence, which brings about understanding. Jesus' first-century, eye-witness biographers provided credible evidence of His life and teachings, the substantiation we need to have faith in Him.

---

[74] "What was from the beginning" = Jesus

[75] "The Word of Life" = Jesus

[76] "The eternal life" = Jesus

[77] 1 John 1:1-3 NASU

[78] God did not require His prophets to compile an exhaustive written account of their activities. Neither Abraham nor Elijah wrote Scripture, yet both remained renowned prophets (Genesis 20:1-7; 1 Kings 18:36). Lesser-known prophets who did not provide written records include Abel (Luke 11:49-51), Ahijah (1 Kings 11:29), Enoch (Jude 14), Jehu (1 Kings 16:1-13), Obed (2 Chronicles 15:8), and others.

[79] Hebrews 11:3 NASU; *Noúmen* (nŏú-mĕn, νοοῦμεν), the Greek word translated "we understand," forms the first person plural present active indicative of the infinitive *noĕo* (nŏ-ĕ́-ō, νοέω), which means "to think carefully."

As John explained, "these have been written so that you may believe."[80]

> *Faith is the **substantiation** of things being hoped for,*
> *the conviction of things not seen.*
> (Hebrews 11:1 BT)

Critical Thinking

Substantiation, God's first factor of faith, relies on critical thinking. Critical thinking compels a person to base beliefs and behavior on careful *reasoning* founded on

> ➤ Sound *evidence* and
>
> ➤ Intellectual *integrity*.[81]

Though many associate critical thinking only with the sciences, we apply it to all facets of life. The quality of our material life depends on the quality of our thought process, that is, how well we utilize critical thinking. Through critical thinking we determine our daily actions by considering substantiated facts (knowledge) coupled with anticipated consequences. Imagine the dreadful quality of life you would have if you did not exercise that type of critical thinking – constantly.

For example, reasoning from sound evidence you compiled every day of your life, you substantiated gravity as a fact some time ago. When you awake from sleep, your intellectual integrity allows you to anticipate the consequence of gravity's existence. Instead of *rolling* out of bed, you demonstrate knowledge and conviction (trusting action) of gravity's effect by planting your feet on the floor, standing up, and walking.

---

[80] John 20:31 NASU

[81] Intellectual integrity – To maintain intellectual integrity, one must remain 1) objective, 2) unslanted by preconceptions or biases, 3) free of contradictory beliefs, and 4) without self-deception.

Likewise, the process we apply to spiritual matters regulates the quality of our spiritual knowledge, spiritual understanding, and spiritual life. Bear in mind the critical thinking process of the spiritual heroes discussed earlier. While maintaining intellectual integrity, they based their behavior on sound evidence regarding what they knew about God, having carefully reasoned their conclusions concerning His power and character.

- Abraham, "having *reasoned* that God also has power to raise a person from the dead,"[82] concluded that God could bring Isaac back to life in order to build Abraham's descendants into a "great nation,"[83] as He had committed.

- Shadrach, Meshach, and Abed-nego carefully *reasoned* and replied to the Babylonian king, "Our God whom we serve is able to deliver us from the furnace of blazing fire … but even if He does not … we are not going to serve your gods."[84]

- Daniel, after contemplating the challenge to his faith,[85] *reasoned* he would rather face the lions than defer to his superior's command for him to cease communication with God for thirty days.

God expects us to apply critical thinking as we consider His history with mankind, His power, and His love. Doing so will lead us to determine, beyond doubt, that He exists, He created all physical reality, and He will keep His promises.

---

[82] Hebrews 11:19 BT
[83] Genesis 12:2 NASU; Genesis 17:4-6
[84] Daniel 3:17-18 NASU
[85] Daniel 6:7,10

***

<u>Contemplation Points</u>

- Do you exercise critical thinking when determining your spiritual beliefs and spiritual behavior?

    a. If so, explain why.

    b. If not, explain why not.

Jesus: Perfect Critical Thinker

Verbal Ambush

Jesus' critical thinking rendered His enemies unable to outwit Him. The passage below illustrates the extent to which religious leaders attempted to discredit Him and how He thwarted their effort.

***

At that point, the Pharisees[86] left and took counsel regarding how they might trap Him in His reasoning.

Then they sent their disciples to Him together with the Herodians,[87] saying, "Teacher, we know that You are honest and truthfully teach the way of God. And no one sways You, because You do not pay attention to the status of people. So tell us, what do You think? Is it lawful to pay poll tax[88] to Caesar, or not?"

Now, knowing their wickedness, Jesus said, "Why are <u>you</u>[89] trying to trap Me? Hypocrites. Show Me the coin for the poll tax."

---

[86] Pharisees – For information concerning the Pharisee sect of the Jews, see "Glossary."

[87] Herodians – Among historians, only Matthew and Mark mention Herodians. Although their identity remains uncertain, they may have represented the family of Herod Antipas, Roman Tetrarch of Galilee, who had traveled to Jerusalem to attend the Passover celebration (Luke 23:4-12).

[88] Poll tax – an annual tax of one denarius the Roman Empire required of its subjects until they reached the age of 65, males from age 14 and females from age 12 (Edersheim, Sketches of Jewish Social Life, 1881, pp. 53-54). However, Roman citizens did not have to pay the poll tax.

[89] To convey the intent of the Greek text, the BT (Bagby Translation) marks you and your with a double underscore when plural (i.e., <u>you</u>, <u>your</u>). For additional information regarding the BT's use of the double underscore, see "Appendix 5: Bagby Translation (BT)," subheading "You and Your."

Then they brought a denarius[90] to Him.

And He said to them, "Whose image and inscription is this?"

They said to Him, "Caesar's."

Then He said to them, "So then, give back to Caesar that which is Caesar's and to God that which is God's."

After hearing this, they were amazed, and leaving Him they went home.[91]

---

[90] Denarius – a small, silver Roman coin that amounted to a day's wages for a common laborer in first-century Judea (Matthew 20:2)
[91] Matthew 22:15-22 BT

Front of an "Emperor Tiberius" Denarius (Minted 20 A.D.)

Figure 1 - 1 (C. Bagby Collection)

Back of an "Emperor Tiberius" Denarius (Minted 20 A.D.)

Figure 1 - 2 (C. Bagby Collection)

Man-Made Religion

Jesus silenced Jewish leaders who promoted doctrines of human origin. He demanded they apply critical thinking to their spiritual life so they could correct their hypocritical religious teachings. Consider His response to the Pharisees and scribes who challenged His disregard for their man-made theological traditions.

***

Then, some Pharisees and scribes from Jerusalem approached Jesus, saying, "Why do Your disciples neglect the tradition of the elders? For they do not wash their hands when they eat bread."[92]

Countering, He said to them, "And, why do you neglect the command of God for the sake of your tradition? For God said, 'Value your father and your mother,'[93] *and 'The one who berates his father or mother should be put to death.'*[94]

"Yet you say, 'Whoever says to his father or his mother, "Whatever I have from which you might have benefited has been pledged as an offering to God," will not be required to provide financial assistance to his father.' In so doing, you negate the Word of God for the sake of your tradition.

---

[92] "Do not wash their hands" – This ceremonial washing had nothing to do with physical sanitation or God's instructions, but related to man-made spiritual cleansing rituals imposed by Pharisees, who required everyone to rinse their hands with water prior to or following certain activities. The Pharisees condemned those who did not comply with their religious traditions of human origin.

[93] Exodus 20:12; Deuteronomy 5:16

[94] Exodus 21:17; Leviticus 20:9

"Hypocrites. Isaiah prophesied accurately concerning <u>*you*</u>*, saying, 'These people value Me with their lips, yet their heart is far away from Me. But they worship Me in vain, teaching the commandments of men as doctrines.'"*[95]

Critical-Thinking Scribe

In Jerusalem, a week or so before Jesus' crucifixion, another group of Pharisees came to Him in the Temple, having heard He had dumbfounded their rivals,[96] the Sadducees.[97] One of those Pharisees, a scribe,[98] demonstrated how God expects us to employ our intellect when considering the writings of His prophets. Having applied critical thinking,[99] that Pharisaic scribe perceived that Jesus' teaching remained consistent with the Scriptures. Exercising intellectual integrity,[100] the scribe credited Him so.

---

[95] Matthew 15:1-9 BT; The final sentence contains a reference to Isaiah 29:13.

[96] Matthew 22:34

[97] Sadducee – For information concerning the Sadducee sect of the Jews, see "Glossary."

[98] Scribes – also referred to as *lawyers,* in relation to the Law of Moses and the religious traditions of the Jewish elders (Matthew 22:35; Luke 7:30; 10:25; 11:45-46,52; 14:3); For more information concerning scribes, see "Glossary."

[99] Critical thinking occurs when one bases beliefs and behavior on the exercise of careful reasoning founded on sound evidence and intellectual integrity.

[100] Intellectual integrity – To maintain intellectual integrity, one must remain 1) objective, 2) unslanted by preconceptions or biases, 3) free of contradictory beliefs, and 4) without self-deception.

***

One of the scribes came and heard them arguing, and recognizing that He had answered them well, asked Him, "What commandment is the foremost of all?"

Jesus answered, "The foremost is, 'Hear, O Israel! The Lord our God is one Lord; and you shall love the Lord your God with all your heart, and with all your soul, and with all your mind, and with all your strength.'[101] The second is this, 'You shall love your neighbor as yourself.'[102] There is no other commandment greater than these."

The scribe said to Him, "Right, Teacher; You have truly stated that He is One, and there is no one else besides Him; and to love Him with all the heart and with all the understanding and with all the strength, and to love one's neighbor as himself is much more than all burnt offerings and sacrifices."

When Jesus saw that he had **answered intelligently,**[103] *He said to him, "***You are not far from the kingdom of God.***"*[104]

---

[101] Deuteronomy 6:4-5

[102] Leviticus 19:18

[103] "Intelligently" – *Nounechós* (nŏün-ĕk-ős, νουνεχῶς), the Greek adverb rendered "intelligently" by the NASU translators in Mark 12:34, forms a compound word. The first part of the term, *noún* (nŏůn, voῦv), refers to the intellectual faculty of reasoning, thinking, perceiving, and deciding (i.e., intelligence). The second part, *echós* (ĕk-ős, εχώς), denotes "having, possessing, holding." Mark explained that this scribe had answered Jesus as one "having intelligence" (i.e., intelligently). In contrast, the scribe's Pharisaic peers and their rival Sadducees, although similarly intelligent, had not *conducted* themselves intelligently as did the scribe. Instead, they posed "foolish and ignorant speculations" (2 Timothy 2:23 NASU) as they attempted to discredit Jesus. To the Sadducees Jesus replied, "You do not understand the Scriptures or the power of God" (Mark 12:24 NASU).

[104] Mark 12:28-34 NASU

***

Contemplation Point

When you last discussed your faith, would Mark (one of God's prophets) have said you conversed intelligently, as he said of the scribe who responded to Jesus (Mark 12:34)?

1. If so, explain why.

2. If not, what action will you take to improve how you discuss your faith with others?

Things Being Hoped For (*Elpidzoménon*)

*Faith is the substantiation **of things being hoped for**,*
the conviction of things not seen.
(Hebrews 11:1 BT)

Elpidzoménon (ĕl-pĭ-dzŏ-mḗ-nōn),[105] the Greek word translated "of things being hoped for," forms the present participle genitive[106] case of the infinitive[107] *elpídzo* (ĕl-pĭ-dzō),[108] which means "to anticipate something with **complete** confidence."

Accordingly, the hope guaranteed by God carries no doubt, for He has provided the means to corroborate "the things being hoped for." Christians possessing the faith God described in Hebrews 11:1 know "the things being hoped for" exist, for they have examined credible evidence to *substantiate* God's history with mankind, His power, His love, and His trustworthiness to follow through on what He has promised.

Paul confirmed God's provision of substantiating evidence when he wrote to the Christians in Rome,

> *Since the creation of the world His* [God's][109] *invisible attributes, His eternal power and divine nature, have been clearly seen, being **understood through what has been made**.*[110]

While Creation substantiates the divine nature of the Creator, Jesus' deity substantiates His ability to keep promises made to those

---

[105] *Elpidzoménon* (ĕl-pĭ-dzŏ-mḗ-nōn), ἐλπιζομένων
[106] Genitive case – The Greek grammatical genitive case denotes possession, or a relation similar to possession, as in "a son **of** David" (Matthew 1:1 BT).
[107] Infinitive – a verb form with no indication of person, number, mood, or tense (Examples of infinitives include *to eat, to run,* and *to swim.*)
[108] *Elpídzo* (ĕl-pĭ-dzō), ἐλπίζω
[109] The author added [God's] to clarify the context.
[110] Romans 1:20 NASU

who place their faith in Him,[111] to deliver the "things being hoped for." Consider the following list, which provides a sampling of commitments made by Jesus.

- *Everyone who beholds the Son and believes in Him will have eternal life, and I Myself will raise him up on the last day.*[112]

- *I am the resurrection and the life; he who believes in Me will live even if he dies, and everyone who lives and believes in Me will never die.*[113]

- *In My Father's house are many dwelling places; if it were not so, I would have told you; for I go to prepare a place for you. If I go and prepare a place for you, I will come again and receive you to Myself, that where I am, there you may be also.*[114]

- *Rejoice and be glad, because your reward in the Heavens*[115] *will be great ....* "[116]

---

[111] Matthew 19:29; John 12:26; 1 Peter 1:3-5; 2 Timothy 2:11-12; James 1:12; and others
[112] John 6:40 NASU
[113] John 11:25-26 NASU
[114] John 14:2-3 NASU
[115] New Testament writers utilized both "heaven" and "heavens" synonymously to communicate the same thing, making no distinction in meaning between the singular and plural forms of the word. To remain as closely parallel to the words originally penned as practical, the BT (Bagby Translation) employs the plural *heavens* each time a writer utilized the plural form of the word in his Greek text. For example, passages within Matthew where such instances occur include Matthew 3:2,16,17; 4:17; 5:3,10,12,16,19,20; 6;1,9; 7:11,21; 8:11; 10:7,32,33; 11:11,12; 12:50; 13:11,24,31,33,44,45,47,52; 16:17,19; 18:1,3,4,10,14,19,23; 19:12,14,21,23; 20:1; 22:2; 23:13; 24:29,36; 25:1.
[116] Matthew 5:12 BT

Conviction (*Élengchos*)

Faith is the substantiation of things being hoped for,
*the **conviction** of things not seen.*
(Hebrews 11:1 BT)

Avoid thinking you have achieved faith by building spiritual knowledge alone. In His definition, God clarifies that the nature of faith goes beyond the intellect and logic that result in the substantiation of facts. To possess God-defined faith, a you must act on what you have come to know.

When substantiated facts became *working* knowledge, ancient writers of Greek used the word *élengchos* (é-lĕng-kŏs) to describe the outcome,[117] here translated "conviction."[118] Conviction (trusting action) must accompany substantiation (knowledge) to produce the faith God expects of us.

Conviction[119] requires follow-through, reasonably justified by confirmed facts. It demands never shrinking back in doubt. As God's prophet instructed his readers at the end of Hebrews chapter 10,

---

[117] *Élengchos* (é-lĕng-kŏs), ἔλεγχος, nominative singular masculine noun

[118] In lieu of the word "conviction," some translators have utilized terms such as "evidence," "proof," "sign," and "certainty." Although those words serve as suitable translations within other contexts, none of them effectively clarifies God's definition of faith in the context of Hebrews chapter 11 as His prophet intended in the Greek text.

[119] Conviction – The word "conviction," as used throughout this book, specifically relates to the Greek word *élengchos*, found only in Hebrews 11:1 within the Scriptures. *Élengchos* consists of *trusting actions* based on knowledge (substantiated fact). Take care not to confuse the *conviction* mentioned in Hebrews 11:1 with other definitions of the English word "conviction" related to finding a person guilty.

> *Do not throw away your confidence, which has a great reward. For you have need of endurance, so that when you have **done** the will of God, you may receive what was promised. ... But **we are not of those who shrink back** to destruction, **but of those who have faith** ....*[120]

Immediately following His definition of faith in Hebrews 11:1, God continued with illustrations to demonstrate that conviction stands indispensable to the faith He requires of His people. Consider this sampling of trusting actions (conviction) from the 11th chapter of Hebrews, works of faith[121] carried out by faithful heroes of the past.

- "By faith Abel **offered**" (Hebrews 11:4)

- "By faith Noah ... **prepared** an ark" (Hebrews 11:7)

- "By faith Abraham ... **obeyed** by going out" (Hebrews 11:8)

- "By faith Abraham ... **offered** up Isaac" (Hebrews 11:17)

- "By faith Moses ... **was hidden** for three months by his parents" (Hebrews 11:23)

- "By faith Moses ... **refused** to be called a son of Pharaoh's daughter, choosing rather to endure ill-treatment" (Hebrews 11:24-25)

- "By faith Rahab ... **welcomed** the spies in peace" (Hebrews 11:31)

*Faith is the substantiation of things being hoped for, the **conviction** of things not seen.*
(Hebrews 11:1 BT)

---

[120] Hebrews 10:35-36,39 NASU

[121] Conviction encompasses every "work of faith" (1 Thessalonians 1:2-3; 2 Thessalonians 1:11-12), from obedience to any trusting action based on God's promises.

Of Things Not Seen

Faith is the substantiation of things being hoped for,
*the conviction **of things not seen**.*
(Hebrews 11:1 BT)

A Christian who attains the faith God demands demonstrates conviction that the things God promised exist – the "things not seen," the "things being hoped for." Each trusting action reveals conviction and confirms the possession of authentic faith in God.

God's Objective Perspective of Faith (Summary)

*Faith is the **substantiation** of things being hoped for,*
*the **conviction** of things not seen.*
(Hebrews 11:1 BT)

Substantiation (Knowledge)

According to God, faith roots itself in substantiated facts. God gave us two things to facilitate *our* substantiation of the realities necessary to attain faith in Him – His *Scriptures* and His *Creation*.

God's Scriptures

But know this first of all, that
no ... Scripture is a matter of one's own interpretation, ...
was ever made by an act of human will, but men moved by
the Holy Spirit spoke from God.[122]

***All** Scripture is **inspired** by God and profitable for*
***teaching**, for **reproof**, for **correction**, for **training** ....*[123]

God's Creation

For since the creation of the world His invisible attributes,
His eternal power and divine nature, have been clearly seen,
*being **understood through what has been made** ....*[124]

---

[122] 2 Peter 1:20-21 NASU
[123] 2 Timothy 3:16 NASU
[124] Romans 1:20 NASU

Conviction (Trusting Action)

Substantiation launches conviction, God's second compulsory component of faith. To exhibit conviction, one must do[125] something that displays trust in that which one knows. Allegiant followers of the Almighty, convinced of His trustworthiness due to the facts substantiated through Scripture and Creation, demonstrate conviction by surrendering to Him. They submit[126] to God because they trust Him and His assurance that the "things not seen," the "things being hoped for," await them if only they obey Him.

> *Faith is the **substantiation** of things being hoped for,*
> *the **conviction** of things not seen.*
> (Hebrews 11:1 BT)

***

Contemplation Points

1. What unseen promises of God do you hope to receive (i.e., *confidently* anticipate)?

2. With what trusting action(s) have you demonstrated your conviction that the unseen promises of God truly await?

---

[125] James 2:17-20; Matthew 7:24-27; John 3:36; John 15:9-10
[126] James 4:7; 1 Peter 5:6

CHAPTER 4

....

You of Little Faith

Jesus told a crowd following Him that their worries indicated they had "little faith."[127] Twice He announced to His apostles that they had "little faith."[128] Once He asked His apostle Peter, "You of little faith, why did you hesitate?"[129] How could they lack faith, since they witnessed Jesus' power?

Maybe we should ask ourselves a more relevant question, "Why do so many of *us* struggle to amass more than a little faith?" Or better, "Why do I have so little faith?" Perhaps we have not witnessed Jesus' power as His apostles did, but within the Scriptures we read the history, the substantiation of His power. Have so many of us not read God's Scriptures? Or, have we forgotten what we have read? What causes us to remain content with our "little faith?"

As you read the following stories, watch for your own weakness.

---

[127] Matthew 6:30; Luke 12:28
[128] Matthew 8:26; 16:8
[129] Matthew 14:31 BT

Little Faith of Jesus' Apostles

Why Are You Afraid?

> *Later, when He went into the boat, His disciples followed Him. Now, listen to this, there was a great upsurge in the sea[130] that covered the boat with waves. Nevertheless, He, Himself, slept.*
>
> *Then, going over to Him, they woke Him saying, "Lord, rescue us! We are being completely destroyed!"*
>
> *And, He said to them, "Why are <u>you</u>[131] afraid? **<u>You</u> of little faith**."[132]*
>
> *So then, having risen, He admonished the winds and the sea, and a great calmness came about.[133]*

---

[130] Sea of Galilee

[131] To convey the intent of the Greek text, the BT (Bagby Translation) marks *you* and *your* with a double underscore when plural (i.e., <u>you</u>, <u>your</u>). For additional information regarding the BT's use of the double underscore, see "Appendix 5: Bagby Translation (BT)," subheading "You and Your."

[132] For emphasis, the author has placed selected words in bold font within passages of Scripture quoted in this book.

[133] Matthew 8:23-26 BT

Why Did You Doubt?

Then He immediately made the disciples get into the boat and cross to the other side[134] *ahead of Him. Meanwhile, He sent away the crowds.*

Later, after dismissing the crowds, He went up onto the hill by Himself to pray. Thus, that evening, He was there alone.

Now, the boat was already many stadiums[135] *from the shore, but hindered by treacherous waves, for the wind was against them. At that point, during the fourth watch of the night,*[136] *He came to them, strolling along on the sea.*

Then, after seeing Him walking around on the sea, the disciples were horrified, saying, "It is a ghost!"

And they screamed out in terror.

So then, Jesus immediately spoke to them, saying, "Take courage! It is I! Do not be afraid!"

Now, answering Him, Peter said, "Lord, since[137] *it is You, tell me to come to You on the water!"*

Then He said, "Come!"

And, after stepping down from the boat, Peter walked about on the water and came toward Jesus. However, seeing the strong wind, Peter was afraid.

Then, beginning to sink, he shouted out, saying,

---

[134] "Other side" – other side of the Sea of Galilee

[135] A stadium equaled about .12 miles (.19 kilometers). Both *stadiums* and *stadia* form the plural of stadium.

[136] The fourth watch of the night took place 3:00 a.m. - 6:00 a.m.

[137] Since – The Greek word *ei* (ĕĭ), εἰ, translates as "since" or "if," depending on the context in which a writer used the word. "If" does not sensibly suit the context, because none of them would have stepped out of the boat onto a tumultuous sea to verify whether a phantom or Jesus truly stood in the distant waves. "Since" logically fits the context of Matthew 14:28, for Peter would not have stepped out of the boat into the stormy water without knowing who had told him to do so – Jesus.

"Lord, save me!"

*At that moment, Jesus immediately stretched out His hand and grabbed him, saying to him, "**You of little faith**. Why did you doubt?"*

After that, once they got into the boat, the wind let up.[138]

***

Contemplation Points

As Jesus pulled Peter out of the sea, He asked, "Why did you doubt?"

1. When would Jesus have asked you the same question?

2. Explain why you doubted.

3. How will you avoid doubt in the future?

---

[138] Matthew 14:22-32 BT

Do You Not Even Remember?

Later, the disciples crossed to the other side,[139] but forgot to bring loaves of bread.

Then Jesus said to them, "Watch out for and be on guard against the yeast of the Pharisees and Sadducees."

And, they wondered about this among themselves, saying, "Because we brought no loaves of bread?"[140]

Now, perceiving this, Jesus said, "**You of little faith**. Why are _you_ wondering about this among yourselves, that _you_ have no loaves of bread? Do _you_ not yet understand? Do _you_ not even remember the five loaves of the five thousand[141] and how many wicker baskets full _you_ picked up? Nor even the seven loaves of the four thousand[142] and how many reed baskets full _you_ picked up?"[143]

---

[139] "Other side" – other side of the Sea of Galilee

[140] Unaware that Jesus spoke metaphorically about the yeast (i.e., influence) of the Pharisees and Sadducees, the apostles thought Jesus' reference perhaps had to do with their having forgotten to bring yeasted (leavened) bread with them on the boat. For a definition of "metaphor," see "Glossary." Also, for additional information concerning the Pharisee and Sadducee sects of the Jews, see "Glossary."

[141] Matthew 14:13-21

[142] Matthew 15:32-38

[143] Matthew 16:5-10 BT

Why Were We Not Able?

After they came to the crowd, a man approached Him, falling on his knees and saying, "Lord, have mercy on my son because he is epileptic and suffers horribly, for he often falls into the fire and frequently into the water. So, I brought him to Your disciples, but they were not able to heal him."

Now, responding, Jesus said, "... Bring him here to Me."

Then, Jesus scolded the demon and it came out of the boy, and he was restored to health that moment.

After that, having gone to Jesus privately, the disciples said, "Why were we not able to drive it out?"

*Then He said to them, "**Due to <u>your</u> insufficient faith**. ...."*[144]

_____

[144] Matthew 17:14-20 BT

Substantiation (Knowledge) Factor of Jesus' Apostles

Jesus' apostles,[145] His closest friends, accompanied Him almost always, carefully listened to His teaching and observed dramatic demonstrations of His divine authority. They had the opportunity to know Jesus and His teachings well. Consequently, they most likely achieved a relatively high knowledge factor during their time with Jesus.

---

[145] Apostle – *transliteration* of the Greek word *apóstolos* (ä-pŏ-stŏ-lŏs), ἀπόστολος, a common Greek word describing any delegate. When transliterating, a translator spells out an approximation of the original language's pronunciation of a word, using the alphabet of the second language. Within the Scriptures, "apostles" typically refers to the 12 followers chosen by Jesus to officially represent Him. For lists of the original twelve, see Matthew 10:1-4; Mark 3:13-19; Luke 6:12-16; and Acts 1:13 (which excludes Judas Iscariot, who had died).

***

Contemplation Points

1. God allowed the nation of Israel to fall due to its shameful lack of knowledge. Consider the following statements made by God concerning Israel's disregard for knowledge of Him and His Scriptures.

    a. Isaiah 1:3 NASU[146]

    An ox knows its owner,
    And a donkey its master's manger,
    But Israel does not know,
    My people do not understand.

    b. Isaiah 5:13 NASU

    Therefore My people go into exile
    for their lack of knowledge ....

    c. Hosea 4:6 NASU

    My people are destroyed for lack of knowledge.
    Because you have rejected knowledge,
    I also will reject you ....

2. Would God consider your knowledge of Him and His Scriptures deficient?

    a. If so, what will you do to improve your knowledge factor.

    b. If not, how have you managed to uphold your knowledge factor?

---

[146] NASU (New American Standard Bible Update, 1995 revision). For more information about the NASU, see the copyright page, among the first pages of this book.

Conviction (Trust) Factor of Jesus' Apostles

Jesus' apostles frequently observed His divine capabilities. Nobody had more opportunity to know Him and His teachings. Their knowledge factor would have grown relatively high compared to that of other disciples who lacked such constant contact with Jesus.

Yet, Jesus expressed disappointment in the underdeveloped faith of His chosen twelve. His apostles demonstrated meager *conviction* (trusting actions, works of faith, follow-through) in what they had come to know. Because their trust lagged far behind their knowledge, their faith remained feeble during the three years they traveled with Him.

CHAPTER 5

....

Your Faith is Great

The few individuals of great faith Jesus acknowledged did not include any of His closest followers, but encompassed comparative strangers. Those few understood what Jesus could do and took trusting action based on their knowledge. Coupling their knowledge (substantiated fact) with a high trust factor (conviction, works of faith, follow-through), they exemplified the faith God intends all His people to possess.

> *Faith is the **substantiation** of things being hoped for,*
> *the **conviction** of things not seen.*
> (Hebrews 11:1 BT)[147]

Reflect on the following passages in which believers outside Jesus' inner circle of friends demonstrated great faith.

---

[147] BT (Bagby Translation) designates a passage of Scripture translated by Dr. Chuck Bagby. For more information regarding the BT, see "Appendix 5: Bagby Translation (BT)."

Two Blind Men

> *Then, as Jesus left there, two blind men followed Him shouting and saying, "Have mercy on us, Son of David!"*[148]

> *Now, after going into the house, He was approached by the blind men, and Jesus said to them, "**Do <u>you</u> believe** that I am able to do this?"*

> *They said to Him, "Yes, Lord."*

> *After that, He touched their eyes, saying, "**According to <u>your</u> faith** let it be done to <u>you</u>."*

> *Then their eyes were opened.*[149]

***

<u>*Contemplation Point*</u>

- With what work(s) of faith (trusting action) did the two blind men demonstrate their *conviction* that Jesus could heal them?

---

[148] "Son of David" became a figure of speech synonymous with Messiah. Jews acknowledged Jesus' identity as the Anointed One (Christ, Messiah) by referring to Him as "Son of David" (Matthew 12:23; Matthew 22:42; Mark 12:35; and others). For a discussion of the Father's anointing of Jesus, see the book *Born to Die* (by Chuck Bagby), "Chapter 2 – Kings & Scoundrels: Jesus' Ancestors," heading "The One Called Christ (Matthew 1:1,16-17)," as well as "Chapter 10 – Jesus Fulfills All Righteousness," heading "Spirit of God Descending (Matthew 3:16)." For additional information concerning David, see the book *Born to Die*, "Chapter 2 – Kings & Scoundrels: Jesus' Ancestors," heading "David (Matthew 1:1,6,17)."

[149] Matthew 9:27-30 BT

Canaanite Woman

> *Then, leaving there, Jesus withdrew into the area of Tyre and Sidon.*
>
> *And, listen to this, a Canaanite woman from that region came out shouting, saying, "Show me mercy, Lord, Son of David! My daughter is miserably demonized!"*
>
> *However, He did not answer a word to her. ...*
>
> *After that, as she came, she was bowing before Him, saying, "Lord, help me." ...*
>
> *Finally, Jesus answered and said to her, "Oh, woman.* **Your faith is great**. *Let it be done for you as you desire."*
>
> *And her daughter was cured that moment.*[150]

***

Contemplation Point

- With what work(s) of faith (trusting action) did the Canaanite woman demonstrate her *conviction* that Jesus could heal her daughter?

---

[150] Matthew 15:21-28 BT

Paralyzed Man & Friends

And some men were carrying on a bed a man who was paralyzed; and they were trying to bring him in and to set him down in front of Him. But not finding any way to bring him in because of the crowd, they went up on the roof and let him down through the tiles with his stretcher, into the middle of the crowd, in front of Jesus.

Seeing their faith, He said, "Friend, your sins are forgiven you."

The scribes[151] and the Pharisees began to reason, saying, "Who is this man who speaks blasphemies? Who can forgive sins, but God alone?"

But Jesus, aware of their reasonings, answered and said to them, "Why are you reasoning in your hearts? Which is easier, to say, 'Your sins have been forgiven you,' or to say, 'Get up and walk?' But, so that you may know that the Son of Man[152] has authority on earth to forgive sins," — He said to the paralytic — "I say to you, get up, and pick up your stretcher and go home."

Immediately he got up before them, and picked up what he had been lying on, and went home glorifying God.[153]

---

[151] Scribes – also referred to as *lawyers,* in relation to the Law of Moses and the religious traditions of the Jewish elders (Matthew 22:35; Luke 7:30; 10:25; 11:45-46,52; 14:3); For more information concerning scribes, see "Glossary."

[152] Son of Man – a favorite term Jesus used to refer to Himself (31 times in Matthew, 14 times in Mark, 26 times in Luke, and 13 times in John). Both Daniel 7:13 and Psalm 80:17 present the term within the context of Messianic prophecy.

[153] Luke 5:18-25 NASU

***

<u>*Contemplation Point*</u>

- With what work(s) of faith (trusting action) did the paralyzed man and his friends demonstrate their *conviction* that Jesus could heal him?

Roman Centurion

> *Now, after He* [Jesus][154] *went into Capernaum, a centurion[155] came toward Him pleading with Him and saying, "Lord, my paralyzed servant has been laid down in the house, terribly afflicted.*

> *Then He said to him, "I will come to heal him."*

> *And, responding, the centurion said, "Lord, I am not worthy enough for You to come under my roof. Instead, just say the word and my servant will be cured. For I am also a man under authority, having soldiers under myself. And I tell this one, 'Go,' and he goes; and to another, 'Come,' and he comes; and to my slave, 'Do this,' and he does it."*

> *Now, after hearing this, Jesus marveled and said to those who were following, "I tell you surely, I have **not found this kind of faith in anyone in Israel**. ..."*

> *Then Jesus said to the centurion, "Be on your way. Let it happen just as you have trusted."*

> *Thus his servant was cured that moment.[156]*

---

[154] The author added [Jesus] to clarify the context.

[155] Centurion – a Roman army official who commanded around 100 soldiers in earlier times, but around 80 during Jesus' lifetime on Earth.

[156] Matthew 8:5-13 BT

***

Contemplation Points

1. With what work(s) of faith (trusting action) did the Roman centurion demonstrate his *conviction* that Jesus could heal his paralyzed servant?

2. If Jesus commented on your faith, which of the following statements might He make?

   a. "Your faith is great." (If so, explain why.)

   b. "You of little faith." (If so, explain why.)

CHAPTER 6

....

Assess Your Faith

You have examined the weak faith of Jesus' apostles, as well as the great faith of a few of His other disciples. In addition, you know the two factors God considers critical to the faith He desires us to develop: substantiation (knowledge) and conviction (trust). Now, you'll estimate the level of your own faith, assess which dynamic of faith you need to give more urgent attention, and explore how you can increase your faith by doing so.

Through one of His prophets, God explained (in Hebrews 11:1) that the faith He wants us to possess consists of two components: substantiation (*hupóstasis*)[157] and conviction (*élengchos*).[158] God's definition of faith lends itself to the development of a useful mathematical equation.

---

[157] For an explanation of the Greek word *hupóstasis*, see "Chapter 3 – Faith Defined by God," heading "Faith (*Pístis*)," subheading "Substantiation (*Hupóstasis*)."

[158] For an explanation of the Greek word *élengchos*, see "Chapter 3 – Faith Defined by God," heading "Faith (*Pístis*)," subheading "Conviction (*Élengchos*)."

The Faith Equation

FAITH	=	KNOWLEDGE	×	TRUST
		(Substantiated Fact, Fact-based Belief)		(Conviction, Trusting Action Based on Knowledge, Follow-through)

To make the equation more readily understood, in place of the terms *substantiation* and *conviction*, **knowledge**[159] (the result of substantiation) and **trust** (the basis of conviction) will represent God's two factors of faith.

Knowledge (substantiation) and trust (conviction) share a mutually-dependent multiplicative relationship within faith.[160] No mathematical operation other than multiplication functions logically in the equation – not addition, not subtraction, not division, etc.[161]

---

[159] Knowledge (substantiated fact) serves as one of the factors used by God to define faith in Hebrews 11:1. All of mankind's spiritual knowledge comes from God (Proverbs 2:6; Psalm 119:66,169; 2 Timothy 3:16-17; 2 Peter 1:20-21). A few passages that discuss the criticality of spiritual knowledge include John 8:31-32, 2 Peter 1:5-7, 2 Peter 3:17-18, Colossians 1:9-10, and Romans 10:1-2.

[160] The equation places equal weight on knowledge (substantiation) and trust (conviction). None of God's Scriptures indicate either of these two factors of faith bears greater influence than the other.

[161] For a discussion of the irrational result of the additive equation **knowledge + trust = faith**, see "Appendix 4: The Non-Functional Additive Equation."

Knowledge (Substantiated Fact)

Imagine the intense hunger Jesus experienced after His 40-day fasting retreat in the Judean Desert.[162] In the same situation, how easily would you have given in to Satan's crafty manipulation?

Approaching Him in a devious attempt to appeal to Jesus' ego, Satan feigned,

> *Since[163] you are the Son of God, tell these stones to become bread.*[164]

Jesus answered,

> *It has been written,*

> *"Man will not live on bread alone, but on every **Word** coming out of the **mouth of God**."*[165]

Despite His 40-day fast, Jesus continued to consider the nourishment gleaned from spiritual knowledge[166] more vital than physical sustenance. Knowledge (substantiation) proves so essential to living a godly life that God included it as one of the two factors in His definition of faith.

> *Faith is the **substantiation** of things being hoped for,*
> *the **conviction** of things not seen.*
> (Hebrews 11:1 BT)

---

[162] Matthew 4:1-2; Mark 1:12-13; Luke 4:1-2

[163] "Since" – The Greek word *ei* (ĕĭ), εἰ, translates as "since" or "if," depending on the context in which a writer employs it. Either translation works well in Matthew 4:3.

[164] Matthew 4:3 BT

[165] Matthew 4:4 BT, a reference to Deuteronomy 8:3.

[166] 2 Timothy 3:16-17

Trust (Conviction, Trusting Actions)

To gain the faith God desires us to acquire, we must not only obtain knowledge, but must act on that knowledge. Trusting action (conviction) must accompany knowledge (substantiation) according to God's definition of faith, as He illustrated in each example of faith presented throughout the 11th chapter of Hebrews.[167]

Furthermore, through His prophet James, God stressed the necessity of conviction (trusting action, follow-through). Referring to the second fundamental of faith (conviction) as "works," that is, works of faith,[168] James wrote,

> *If a brother or sister is inadequately clothed and lacking the day's food, but someone tells them, "Go away in peace, warm yourselves and be filled," yet does not give them the body's essentials, what is the benefit? And likewise,* **faith, if it does not have works** [of faith],[169] **is dead** *by itself.*[170]

He went on to explain,

> *Faith without works* [of faith] *is* **useless**.[171]

---

[167] Hebrews 11:4-31

[168] James 2:14-26

[169] The author added [of faith] to clarify the context. For God's use of the term "work of faith," see 1 Thessalonians 1:2-3 NASU and 2 Thessalonians 1:11-12 NASU. (NOTE: If the version you read does not employ the term "work of faith" in these two passages, it contains a paraphrase of the verse instead of a translation. A paraphrase presents human opinion – commentary. A translation precisely renders the language in which a prophet wrote God's Scripture into another language, without integrating human commentary.) For a thorough discussion of works of faith, see "Chapter 7: Works of Merit or Works of Faith?"

[170] James 2:15-17 BT

[171] James 2:20 BT

Then, again James emphasized,

As indeed the body without a spirit is dead, so also, faith without works [of faith] *is* ***dead***.[172]

Reflect on the essence of that last point, "faith without works is dead." Consistent with God's definition of faith in Hebrews 11:1, if one removes conviction (trusting actions, works of faith, follow-through) from substantiation (knowledge), faith ceases to exist.

Faith is the ***substantiation*** *of things being hoped for,*
the ***conviction*** *of things not seen.*
(Hebrews 11:1 BT)

Examine the results of the following *Scriptural Application Test* and *Practical Application Test*. Afterward, decide for yourself whether the faith equation correctly represents God's astute description of faith.

---

[172] James 2:26 BT

Scriptural Application Test

Suppose Robert possesses 50% knowledge[173] (substantiated fact) and 0% trust (conviction, trusting actions, works of faith, follow-through).

$$.50 \text{ knowledge} \times 0 \text{ trust} = 0\% \text{ faith}$$

Multiplying his knowledge factor by his trust factor, the faith equation yields a faith product of 0% for Robert, since his trust factor (works of faith) equals zero. The equation's calculation proves consistent with God's proclamation that, without works of faith (conviction, trusting actions, follow-through), faith remains "useless" – "dead."[174]

The Scriptural Application Test validates the faith equation's fidelity to the definition God advanced in Hebrews 11:1. Yet, will the equation work in your life? Will it pass the following Practical Application Test?

---

[173] Specifically, knowledge God would have us glean from His Scriptures
[174] See James 2:14-26 NASU (Note verses 17, 20, and 26.)

Practical Application Test

Suppose Kayley learns and substantiates one out of twenty things God has made possible to know through study of His Scriptures. Her knowledge factor would amount to 5% (i.e., $1 \div 20 = .05 = 5\%$).

Likewise, when an opportunity occurs for Kayley to carry out a work of faith, four out of five times she confidently acts on her 5% knowledge. Her trust factor calculates to 80% (i.e., $4 \div 5 = .80 = 80\%$).

With knowledge and trust factors estimated, Kayley can calculate the approximate percentage of available faith she possesses by inserting her factors of faith into the equation.

$$.05 \text{ knowledge} \times .80 \text{ trust} = .04 = 4\% \text{ faith}$$

The equation determines that Kayley would have achieved 4% of the faith God has made accessible – a feasible, real-world outcome.

The results of both the Scriptural Application Test and the Practical Application Test confirm the utility of the faith equation derived from Hebrews 11:1. The equation proves sound.

Increasing One's Faith

Like Kayley, Charlie possesses 4% faith (5% knowledge × 80% trust). Even though he possesses the same knowledge and trust factors as Kayley, he does not have to remain at 4% faith forever. Charlie's faith will grow as he increases his knowledge, trust, or both.

1. If Charlie boosts his *trust* factor from 80% to 95%, his faith will have grown from 4% to 4.75%.

   .05 knowledge × .95 trust = .0475 = 4.75% faith

2. However, if he builds his *knowledge* factor from 5% to 10%, his faith will have doubled from 4% to 8%.

   .10 knowledge × .80 trust = .08 = 8% faith

3. Better still, if Charlie improves both factors of faith, raising trust from 80% to 95% and knowledge from 4% to 10%, his faith will have grown from 4% to 9.5%.

   .10 knowledge × .95 trust = .095 = 9.5% faith

KNOWLEDGE ×	**TRUST** =	**FAITH**
(Substantiated Fact, Fact-based Belief)	(Conviction, Trusting Action Based on Knowledge, Follow-through)	(Knowledgeable, Trusting Action)

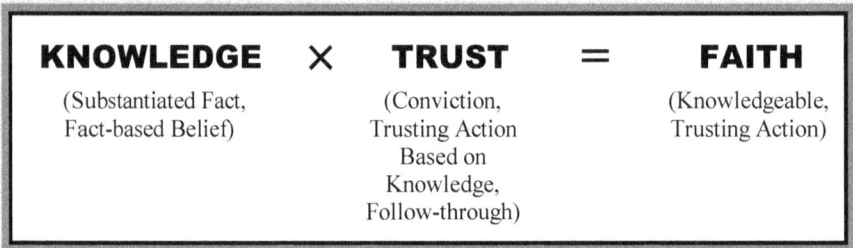

The following graph assumes a beginning faith consisting of 5% knowledge and 80% trust. As you view the graph, beginning at the *bottom*, notice how faith increases as knowledge (substantiation) and trust (conviction) improve together.

INCREASING FAITH

(Begin at bottom)

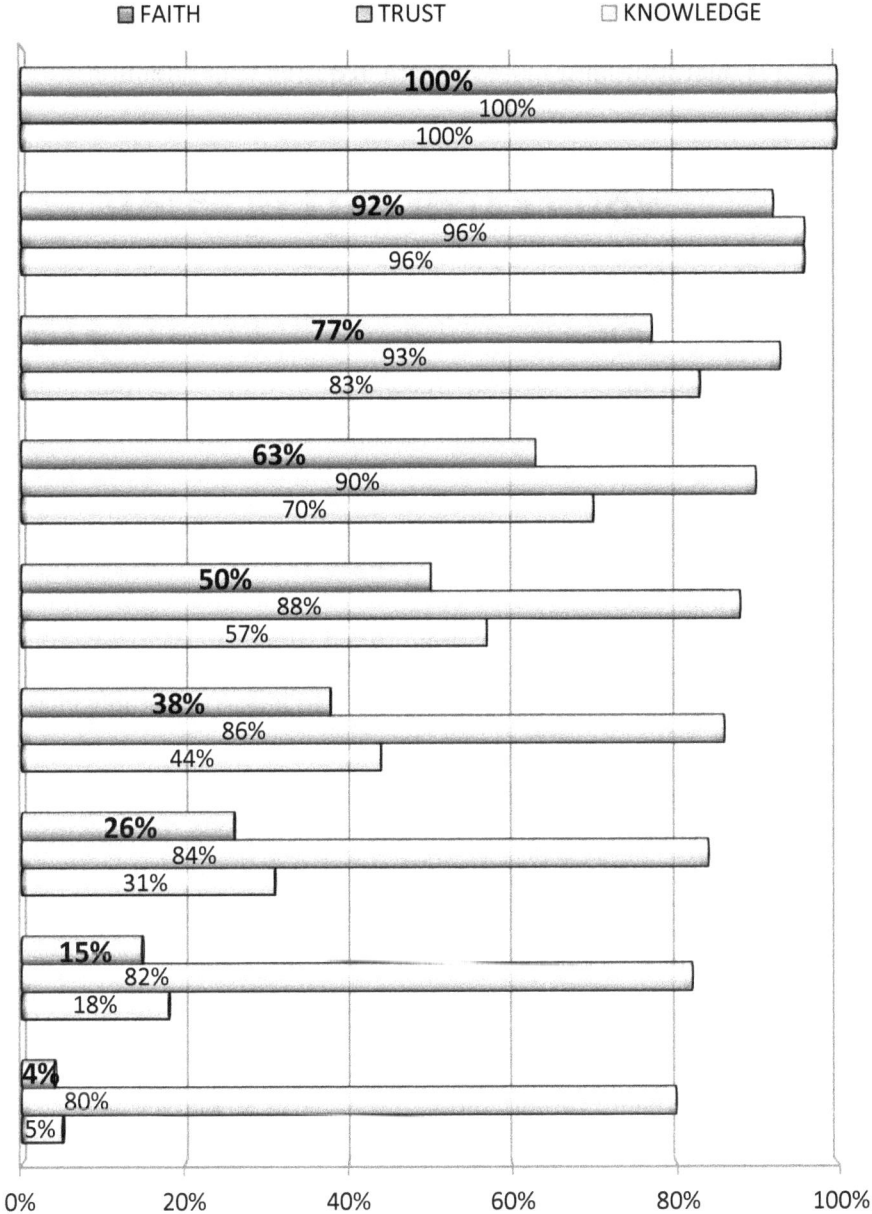

☐ FAITH   ☐ TRUST   ☐ KNOWLEDGE

100%
100%
100%

92%
96%
96%

77%
93%
83%

63%
90%
70%

50%
88%
57%

38%
86%
44%

26%
84%
31%

15%
82%
18%

4%
80%
5%

0%   20%   40%   60%   80%   100%

71

***

Contemplation Point

Assess *your* faith by performing the calculation in the following chart. Although faith remains *virtually unquantifiable*, this exercise will help you determine which factor of faith more urgently requires your attention.

YOUR FAITH CALCULATION

_____% **×** _____% **=** _____%

KNOWLEDGE   **TRUST**   **FAITH**

(Substantiated Fact,   (Conviction,   (Knowledgeable,
Fact-based Belief)   Trusting Action   Trusting Action)
                         Based on
                         Knowledge,
                         Follow-through)

---

1. Estimate your **knowledge factor**, the percentage of the Scriptures you know and understand. Then, insert that number in the chart, above the word KNOWLEDGE. (Although *virtually unquantifiable*, make a generous estimate.)

2. Estimate your **trust factor**, the percentage of times you confidently act on what you know when given the opportunity. Then, insert that number in the chart, above the word TRUST. (Although *virtually unquantifiable*, make a generous estimate.)

3. **Multiply** your knowledge factor by your trust factor.

4. Insert the **product** of the calculation in the chart, above the word FAITH.

5. In which factor of faith did you score lowest, knowledge or trust?

6. How will you ensure that you grow in that area?

CHAPTER 7

....

Works of Faith or Works of Merit?

Disagreement regarding the relationship between works and salvation has divided Christians for ages. Some have misapplied Paul's explanation that God does *not* justify[175] anyone based on works.[176] Others have misrepresented James' affirmation that God will not justify anyone who remains *without* works.[177] Both groups fail to recognize that Paul and James complement one another in their writings, each discussing a different type of work.

---

[175] Justify – to treat as not guilty. When God has *justified* someone, through His mercy and grace He regards that person as *just* (i.e., innocent of wrongdoings) despite past misconduct, because Jesus paid the penalty with His sacrificial crucifixion. Only the compelling blood of an innocent man's voluntary self-sacrifice could bridge the chasm separating a guilty human from God's favor (Hebrews 9:22; Leviticus 17:11).

[176] Ephesians 2 :8-9; Romans 3:28

[177] James 2:14-26

Paul addressed *works of merit* when he denied any connection between salvation and works. He explained that one cannot earn (merit) salvation through one's works.[178]

On the other hand, James examined *works of faith* when he clarified that works do relate to salvation. A Christian must pair trusting action (works of faith, conviction, follow-through) with knowledge of God's promises and His expectations that we demonstrate the faith He described in Hebrews 11:1.

Take care to note the difference between the

- *Works* (*of faith*)[179] James had in mind when he wrote, "a person is justified by works,"[180] and the

- *Works* (*of merit*) to which Paul referred when he wrote, "a man is justified by faith apart from works."[181]

At first reading, Paul and James appear to conflict. However, when one recognizes each addressed a different kind of work,[182] the misconstrued conflict vanishes.

To illustrate that the works of which Paul and James wrote differed in nature, consider their comments regarding Abraham.

---

[178] Specifically, Paul challenged those in the first-century church who taught in error that a Gentile believer must fulfill the old covenant Law of Moses rite of circumcision to merit God's salvation.

[179] Paul *commends* the Christians in Thessalonica for their "work of faith" (not works of merit or works of the Law) in 1 Thessalonians 1:2-3 NASU and 2 Thessalonians 1:11-12 NASU. (NOTE: If the version you read does not employ the term "work of faith" in these two passages, it contains a paraphrase of the verse instead of a translation. A paraphrase presents human opinion – commentary. A translation precisely renders the language in which a prophet wrote God's Scripture into another language, without integrating human commentary.)

[180] James 2:24 BT

[181] Romans 3:28 NASU; Galatians 2:16; Ephesians 2:8-9

[182] As in all study of the Scriptures, one must note the context addressed by the writer. Context, the communication before and after a word or passage, often sheds light on the meaning intended by the writer or speaker.

Concerning works of merit, Paul wrote to the Roman Christians,

For if Abraham was justified by works [of merit],[183] *he has something to boast about, but not before God. For what does the Scripture say? "Abraham* **believed**[184] [had faith in][185] *God, and it was* **credited to him as righteousness.** *"*[186]

Whereas, regarding works of faith, James asked the rhetorical question,

Was not Abraham our father **justified by works** [of faith] *having offered up his son Isaac on the altar?*[187]

---

[183] The author added [of merit] to clarify the context.

[184] Believed – *Epísteusen* (e-pĭs-tĕü-ŏü-sĕn, ἐπίστευσεν), the Greek verb here rendered "believed" by the NASU, forms the third person singular aorist active indicative grammatical construct of its infinitive *pisteúo* (pĭs-tĕǘ-ō, πιστεύω). *Pisteúo* can translate as "to believe (a fact)," "to trust," or "to have faith in," depending on the context in which a writer employed the word. Abraham went beyond believing (i.e., knowing facts). For this reason, "had faith in" (instead of "believed") best suits the context of this sentence. Abraham followed through with works of faith, he did not merely believe a fact. Due to his follow-through on what he knew, his faith "was credited to him as righteousness." As God explained in Hebrews 11:1, faith consists of substantiation (knowledge, substantiated fact) paired with conviction (trusting action, follow-through). Faith becomes complete when one joins fact-based belief (substantiation, knowledge) with works of faith (conviction, trusting actions), as explained in James 2:22.

[185] The author added [had faith in] to provide a more precise translation.

[186] Romans 4:2-3 NASU

[187] James 2:21 BT

Works of Merit

Works of merit (works performed to earn something) differ from the works of faith (conviction, trusting actions, follow-through) God included as one of the two factors of faith listed in Hebrews 11:1. Devoted Christians follow through with *works of faith* to demonstrate their love of God and their trust in His vow to forgive wrongdoings through His mercy. In contrast, misguided individuals perform *works of merit* expecting to earn God's approval, uselessly attempting to obligate Him to save them from eternal punishment.

Christians & God's Law for Israel

In the day of Jesus' apostle Paul, some promoted the mistaken concept that a Christian must earn salvation by performing works God previously required of the Israelites under His old covenant, the Law of Moses. Paul corrected that line of thought when he taught the Roman Christians,

> *Apart from the Law* [of Moses] *the righteousness of God has been manifested, ... even the righteousness of God through faith in Jesus Christ for all those who believe ... being justified*[188]*as a gift by His grace through the redemption which is in Christ Jesus ... so that He would be just and the justifier of the one who has faith in Jesus. ... For we maintain that a man is **justified by faith apart from works of the Law** [of Moses].*[189]

---

[188] Justify – to treat as not guilty. When God has "justified" someone, through His mercy and grace He regards that person as "just" (i.e., innocent of wrongdoings) despite past misconduct, because Jesus paid the penalty through His sacrificial crucifixion. Only the compelling blood of an innocent man's voluntary self-sacrifice could bridge the chasm separating a guilty human from God's favor (Hebrews 9:22; Leviticus 17:11).

[189] Romans 3:21-28 NASU; The author added [of Moses] to clarify the context.

Similarly, Paul reminded Christians in the region of Galatia,

> *A man is **not justified by the works of the Law** [of Moses] but through faith in Christ Jesus ... so that we may be justified by faith in Christ and not by the works of the Law [of Moses] ....*[190]

Furthermore, Paul explained to Christians in the city of Ephesus,

> *For **by grace you have been saved through faith**; and that not of yourselves, it[191] is the gift of God; **not as a result of works** [of merit], so that no one may boast.*[192]

---

[190] Galatians 2:16 NASU; The author added [of Moses] to clarify the context.

[191] The pronoun "it" does not refer to "faith" as the gift of God, but to *salvation*, "by grace you have been **saved** through faith." As a result of a person's demonstration of faith, God graciously rescues him from the dreadful consequence of his sin.

[192] Ephesians 2:8-9 NASU; The author added [of merit] to clarify the context.

Man-made Religious Traditions & Works of Merit

Consider the Pharisee[193] below who thought himself righteous by his own merit.

The Self-Righteous Pharisee

And He [Jesus] *also told this parable to some people who **trusted in themselves** that they were righteous, and viewed others with contempt:*

"Two men went up into the temple to pray, one a Pharisee and the other a tax collector.

The Pharisee stood and was praying this to himself: 'God, I thank You that I am not like other people: swindlers, unjust, adulterers, or even like this tax collector. I fast twice a week; I pay tithes of all that I get.'

But the tax collector, standing some distance away, was even unwilling to lift up his eyes to heaven, but was beating his breast, saying, 'God, be merciful to me, the sinner!'

I tell you, this man went to his house justified rather than the other; for everyone who exalts himself will be humbled, but he who humbles himself will be exalted."[194]

In His old covenant[195] with Israel, God required only one fast

---

[193] For information concerning the Pharisee sect of the Jews, see "Glossary."
[194] Luke 18:9-14 NASU
[195] Old covenant = the Law of Moses; 2 Corinthians 3:14-16; Hebrews 6:19-8:13

each year, on the Day of Atonement[196] (i.e., Yom Kippur). Yet Pharisees, obsessed with religious rituals of their own invention, fasted twice per week, typically each second and fifth day (Monday and Thursday) during the weeks between the Passover[197] and Pentecost, [198] as well as between the Feast of Tabernacles[199] and the Feast of Dedication[200] (i.e., Hanukkah). (Edersheim, The Temple: Its

---

[196] Day of Atonement – an annual day of Israelite fasting, during which specific animal sacrifices prescribed by God took place; In Leviticus 16:29, the Hebrew idiomatic expression "humble your souls" (NASU) refers to fasting. [NOTE: The New International Version and the New Revised Versions render "humble your souls" (a Hebrew idiomatic expression meaning "fast") as "deny yourselves." The King James Version renders it as "afflict your souls."] See also Psalm 35:13; Ezra 8:21; Isaiah 58:3,5; Leviticus 23:27,29,32 for other passages employing "humble" in the context of fasting. For a definition of the term *idiomatic expression*, see "Glossary."

[197] Passover – one of the three annual festivals (Deuteronomy 16:16) for which God commanded adult male Israelites to travel to Jerusalem (optional for other family members). The Passover-day festival, coupled with the seven-day Feast of Unleavened Bread which immediately followed the Passover, served as an eight-day memorial celebration of God's liberation of the Israelites from Egyptian captivity.

[198] Pentecost – also called Feast of Weeks, took place the 50th day after Passover; God listed Pentecost among the three annual festivals (Deuteronomy 16:16) for which He commanded adult male Israelites to travel to Jerusalem (optional for other family members). Pentecost celebrated the end of the annual grain harvest.

[199] Feast of Tabernacles – also called Feast of Booths; God listed the Feast of Tabernacles/Booths among the three annual festivals (Deuteronomy 16:16) for which He commanded adult male Israelites to travel to Jerusalem (optional for other family members). The Feast of Tabernacles/Booths commemorated the 40 years God had Israel wander in the wilderness due to their lack of faith in His promise to lead them to victory over the evil nations occupying the land He had committed to Abraham's descendants.

[200] Feast of Dedication – a man-made religious festival, also known as *Hanukkah*, which originated as an outcome of the Jewish Maccabean Revolt against the rule of the Greek Seleucid Empire. It commemorated the 165 B.C. rededication of the Temple and its altar by Judas Maccabaeus, following their desecration in 167 B.C. by Antiochus Epiphanes, the king of the Seleucid Empire.

Ministry and Services, 1874, p. 167) Hence, this Pharisee boasted to God, "I fast *twice* a week."[201]

In His parable, Jesus grouped this Pharisee among those "people who *trusted in themselves* that they were righteous."[202] Pharisees mistakenly believed their strict adherence to the religious traditions fabricated by their ancestors kept them spiritually pure. Convinced he had *earned* God's goodwill through his works of merit, the Pharisee in Jesus' story ridiculed the humble tax collector. Jesus strongly condemned the nature of the Pharisees' religious thought and practice.[203]

FAITH $\neq$ **KNOWLEDGE** $\times$ **WORKS OF MERIT**

(Substantiated Fact, Fact-based Belief)

***

Contemplation Points

1. Have you ever found yourself trying to earn your way to Heaven by performing works of merit?

2. If so,

   a. Describe some of those works.

   b. What led you to attempt to earn your way to Heaven?

---

[201] Luke 18:12 NASU
[202] Luke 18:9 NASU
[203] Matthew 15:1-9; 16:6-12; 23:13-33; Mark 7:1-13; 8:15; Luke 12:1

Paul and Works of Faith

Paul declared no *work* (*of merit*) results in a Christian's justification/salvation. Yet, he commended the Christians in the city of Thessalonica for their *work of faith*. Paul wrote,

> *We give thanks to God always for all of you, making mention of you in our prayers; constantly bearing in mind your **work of faith** and labor of love and steadfastness of hope in our Lord Jesus Christ in the presence of our God and Father ....*[204]

> *We pray for you always, that our God will count you worthy of your calling, and fulfill every desire for goodness and the **work of faith** with power, so that the name of our Lord Jesus will be glorified in you, and you in Him, according to the grace of our God and the Lord Jesus Christ.*[205]

---

[204] 1 Thessalonians 1:2-3 NASU; NOTE: If the version you read does not employ the term "work of faith" in this passage, it contains a paraphrase of the verse instead of a translation. A paraphrase presents human opinion – commentary. A translation precisely renders the language in which a prophet wrote God's Scripture into another language, without integrating human commentary.

[205] 2 Thessalonians 1:11-12 NASU; NOTE: If the version you read does not employ the term "work of faith" in this passage, it contains a paraphrase of the verse instead of a translation. A paraphrase presents human opinion – commentary. A translation precisely renders the language in which a prophet wrote God's Scripture into another language, without integrating human commentary.

James and Works of Faith

Some first-century Christians incorrectly taught *works of faith* have no relevance to salvation. In response, James, one of God's prophets, explained the necessary combination of knowledge and works of faith (conviction, trusting actions, follow-through) required to possess the faith God desires of us. Commenting on works of faith (not works of merit), he wrote,[206]

> *What is the benefit, my brethren, if someone says he has faith, but **does not have works** [of faith]?*[207] ***Is that faith able to save him?***
>
> *If a brother or sister is inadequately clothed and lacking the day's food, but someone tells them, "Go in peace, warm yourselves and be filled," yet does not give them the body's essentials, what is the benefit?*
>
> *And likewise, **faith**, if it **does not have works** [of faith], is **dead** by itself. ...*
>
> *Demonstrate your faith to me without works [of faith], and I will demonstrate faith to you by means of my works [of faith].*

---

[206] In this passage, James did not contradict Paul's statement in Ephesians 2:8-9, "For by grace you have been saved through faith; and that not of yourselves, it is the gift of God; not as the result of works [of merit]." In fact, James supplemented Paul's point, clarifying that works [of faith] make faith complete (James 2:22) and "belief without works [of faith] is useless" and "dead" (James 2:17,20 BT; See also Matthew 7:24-29).

[207] The author added [of faith] to clarify the context. See also 1 Peter 1:17-19 (Note verse 17.); John 5:28-29; Romans 2:4-8 (Note verses 6-7.); 2 Corinthians 5:10; Titus 2:6-8 (Note verse 7.)

You believe[208] [the fact] *that God is one. You do well. The demons also believe*[209] *and tremble. But are you willing to acknowledge, O witless person, that* **belief**[210] **without works** [of faith] **is useless***?*

Was not **Abraham** *our father* **justified by works** [of faith] *having offered up his son Isaac on the altar?*[211] *You*[212] *see that* **belief was working together with his works** [of faith]*, and the works completed his faith, and the Scripture was fulfilled that says, "Then Abraham had faith in God, and it was credited to him as righteousness,"*[213] *and he was called*

---

[208] *Pisteúeis* (pǐs-těǘ-ěǐs, πιστεύεις), the Greek verb here rendered "believe," forms the second person singular present indicative active grammatical construct of its infinitive *pisteúo* (pǐs-těǘ-ō, πιστεύω), which can translate as "to believe (a fact)," "to trust," or "to have faith in," depending on the context in which a writer employed the word. "Believe" (instead of "trust" or "have faith in") best suits the immediate context of this sentence due to the direct comparison drawn in the second half of the sentence to demons, who also believe the fact that God is one.

[209] *Pisteúousin* (pǐs-těǘ-ǒü-sǐn, πιστεύουσιν), the Greek verb here rendered "believe," forms the third person singular present indicative active grammatical construct of its infinitive *pisteúo* (pǐs-těǘ-ō, πιστεύω), which can translate as "to believe (a fact)," "to trust," or "to have faith in," depending on the context in which a writer employed the word. "Believe" (instead of "trust" or "have faith in") best suits the immediate context of this sentence, given that demons do not place their trust in God and hence do not place their faith in Him.

[210] *Pístis* (pǐs-tǐs, πίστις), the Greek noun (nominative singular feminine) here rendered "belief," can translate as "belief (fact-based knowledge)," "trust," or "faith," depending on the context in which a writer employed the word. "Belief" (instead of "trust" or "faith") best suits the context of this sentence, for faith, without works of faith, remains merely belief of a fact. Faith becomes complete (James 2:22) when one joins *belief* (fact-based knowledge, substantiation) with *works of faith* (trusting action, conviction).

[211] See Genesis 22:1-19 for the story of Abraham's sacrifice of Isaac.

[212] To convey the intent of the Greek text, the BT (Bagby Translation) marks *you* and *your* with a double underscore when plural (i.e., you, your). For additional information regarding the BT's use of the double underscore, see "Appendix 5: Bagby Translation (BT)," subheading "You and Your."

[213] Genesis 15:6

> *a friend of God.*[214] <u>*You*</u> *see that a person is justified*[215] ***by works*** [of faith] ***and not by belief***[216] ***alone****.*
>
> *And in the same way, was not Rahab, the prostitute,* ***justified by works*** [of faith] *when she showed hospitality to the messengers and sent them out on another route?*[217]
>
> *As indeed the body without a spirit is dead, so also,* ***faith without works*** [of faith] ***is dead****.*[218]

Submissive followers of God show their conviction by following through with works of faith, demonstrating their trust in Him to mercifully forgive their wrongdoings as He pledged. Christians who possess the faith God described in Hebrews 11:1 live faithfully through trusting actions (conviction, works of faith, follow-through). In the *works of faith* context, James wrote, "You see that a person is justified by works and not by belief alone."[219]

---

[214] Isaiah 41:8-9; 2 Chronicles 20:7

[215] Justify – to treat as not guilty. When God has "justified" someone, through His mercy and grace He regards that person as "just" (i.e., innocent of wrongdoings) despite past misconduct, because Jesus paid the penalty with His sacrificial crucifixion. Only the compelling blood of an innocent man's voluntary self-sacrifice could bridge the chasm separating a guilty human from God's favor (Hebrews 9:22; Leviticus 17:11).

[216] *Písteuos* (pĭs-tĕü-ōs, πίστεως), the Greek noun (genitive, singular, feminine) here rendered "belief," can translate as "belief (fact-based belief)," "trust," or "faith," depending on the context in which a writer employed the word. "Belief" best suits the context of this sentence, for James stresses when a person pairs fact-based belief with trusting works of faith (James 2:24), the person has demonstrated the faith through which God extends His mercy and grace, granting justification and salvation (Romans 5:1-2; Ephesians 2:8).

[217] See Joshua 2:1-24 for the story of Rahab.

[218] James 2:14-26 BT

[219] James 2:24 BT; 1 Peter 1:17; John 3:36; John 15:9-10

Works of Faith by Heroes of Faith

God paired *conviction* (trusting action, follow-through) with *substantiation* (fact-based knowledge) in His Hebrews 11:1 faith definition. Immediately thereafter, He provided a series of real-life examples of trusting actions (conviction, works of faith, follow-through). The following God-given examples illustrate the working faith a person must have to become a beneficiary of God's gracious forgiveness of sins.

> ***By faith*** *Abel* **offered** *to God a better sacrifice than Cain, through which he obtained the testimony that he was righteous ...*

> ***By faith*** *Noah, being warned by God about things not yet seen, in reverence* **prepared** *an ark for the salvation of his household ...*

> ***By faith*** *Abraham, when he was called,* **obeyed** *by going out to a place which he was to receive for an inheritance; and he went out, not knowing where he was going.* ***By faith*** *he* **lived as an alien** *in the land of promise, as in a foreign land, dwelling in tents with Isaac and Jacob, fellow heirs of the same promise ...*

> ***By faith*** *Abraham, when he was tested,* **offered** *up Isaac, and he who had received the promises ... considered that God is able to raise people even from the dead ...*

> ***By faith*** *Moses, when he was born,* **was hidden** *for three months by his parents ... and they were not afraid of the king's edict.*

> ***By faith*** *Moses, when he had grown up,* **refused** *to be called the son of Pharaoh's daughter, choosing rather to endure ill-treatment with the people of God than to enjoy the passing pleasures of sin ...* ***By faith*** *he* **left** *Egypt, not fearing the wrath of the king; for he endured, as seeing Him who is unseen.* ***By faith*** *he* **kept** *the Passover and the sprinkling of the blood, so that he who destroyed the firstborn would not*

touch them.

*   **By faith** they **passed through** the Red Sea as though they were passing through dry land; and the Egyptians, when they attempted it, were drowned.*

*   **By faith** the walls of Jericho fell down after they had been **encircled** for seven days.*

*   **By faith** Rahab the harlot did not perish along with those who were disobedient, after she had **welcomed** the spies in peace.*

*   And what more shall I say? For time will fail me if I tell of Gideon, Barak, Samson, Jephthah, of David and Samuel and the prophets, who **by faith conquered** kingdoms, **performed** acts of righteousness ... **shut** the mouths of lions, **quenched** the power of fire, **escaped** the edge of the sword ... **put** foreign armies **to flight**. ... And all these ... gained approval through their faith ....[220]*

FAITH	=	KNOWLEDGE	×	TRUST
		(Substantiated Fact, Fact-based Belief)		(Works of Faith, Trusting Action Based on Knowledge, Conviction, Follow-through)

---

[220] Hebrews 11:4-39 NASU

***

Contemplation Point

- In the spaces below, write a sentence describing one of your works of faith, as though listed in the 11th chapter of Hebrews.
- Bear in mind, faith = knowledge × trust [works of faith, trusting actions, conviction, follow-through].
- If you cannot think of a work of faith to insert, describe one you wish you could insert as yours.
- Take your time. This point requires careful thought.

By faith, _____ (←Insert your name, then describe a trusting action in the lines that follow.→)

_____

_____

_____

_____

_____

_____

_____

_____

_____

_____

_____

_____

··

CHAPTER 8

Repentance: A Christian's First Work of Faith

> *Now, in those days, John the Immerser*[221] *came proclaiming in the Judean Desert, saying, "**Repent**, for the Kingdom of the Heavens*[222] *has come near."*[223]

Not long thereafter, Herod Antipas,[224] Tetrarch[225] of Galilee, beheaded John the Immerser.

> *From that time forward, **Jesus** began to proclaim and to say, "**Repent**, for the Kingdom of the Heavens has come near."*[226]

---

[221] Immerser – *Baptistés* (Bäp-tĭs-tås, βαπτιστὴς), the Greek word translated "Immerser," often finds itself *transliterated* as "Baptist," instead of *translated* precisely as "Immerser." For more information about John, see the book *Born to Die* (by Chuck Bagby), "Chapter 8 – The Desert Prophet." For a discussion of the origin of the word "Baptist," see *Born to Die*, "Chapter 8 – The Desert Prophet," heading "They Were Immersed (Matthew 3:6)."

[222] New Testament writers utilized both "heaven" and "heavens" synonymously to communicate the same thing, making no distinction in meaning between the singular and plural forms of the word. To remain as closely parallel to the words originally penned as practical, the BT (Bagby Translation) employs the plural *heavens* each time a writer utilized the plural form of the word in the Greek text.

[223] Matthew 3:1-2 BT

[224] Herod Antipas – a son of Herod the Great

[225] Tetrarch – "Ruler of a Fourth" (Tetrarchy – one fourth of a Roman client kingdom or province)

[226] Matthew 4:17 BT

Repent

John the Immerser and Jesus proclaimed their divine message to anyone who would listen, announcing, "Repent, for the Kingdom of the Heavens has come near."[227]

Most define "to repent" something like "to feel regret" or "to be sorry." Nevertheless, the repentance God demands of us goes beyond an emotional regret or verbal declaration of sorrow. Only from His Scriptures can we learn what God meant when He commanded *repentance*.

Repentance (Reasoned, Deliberate Change)

The Greek[228] word here[229] translated "repent," *metanoeíte* (mě-tä-nŏ-ĕí-tě),[230] appears as a conjugated[231] form of the infinitive[232] *metanoéo* (mět-ä-nŏ-ĕ́-ō).[233] *Metanoéo* combines two Greek words; *metá*,[234] which denotes "after," and *noéo*,[235] meaning "to think carefully."

---

[227] Matthew 3:1-2; 4:17 BT

[228] The authors of the New Testament books and correspondence wrote their works in Greek, which served as an international language during the first century A.D. due to the enduring Hellenistic (Greek) influence of Alexander the Great's vast conquests three centuries earlier as he expanded his Macedonian Empire. By writing in Greek, New Testament authors effectively communicated within the Roman-Empire, as well as non-Roman Mediterranean cultures.

[229] Matthew 3:1-2; 4:17 BT

[230] *Metanoeíte* (mě-tä-nŏ-ĕí-tě), μετανοεῖτε

[231] Conjugated – A conjugated form of an infinitive reflects the number, person, tense, etc. that a writer intends to communicate.

[232] Infinitive – a verb form with no indication of person, number, mood, or tense (Examples of infinitives include *to eat*, *to run*, and *to swim*.)

[233] *Metanoeo* (mě-tä-nŏ-ĕ́-ō), μετανοέω

[234] *Metá* (mě-tá), μετά

[235] *Noéo* (nŏ-ĕ́-ō), νοέω

The repentance John and Jesus proclaimed involves changing *thoughts* and *behavior* as the result of deliberate consideration. It surpasses a feeling of sorrow.

Not Merely Saying "Sorry"

Jesus' apostle Paul wrote to the Christians in the city of Corinth,

> *I now rejoice, not that you were made **sorrowful**, but that you were made sorrowful to the point of **repentance**.*[236]

The Greek word here translated "you were made sorrowful," *elupéthete* (ĕ-lü-pá-thā-tĕ),[237] appears as a conjugated form of the infinitive *lupéo* (lü-pĕ́-ō),[238] which means "to make sad." It indicates distress or grief caused as the result of a past occurrence.

Neither John nor Jesus warned those who practiced sin to *feel sorry*, but to modify their lifestyle. John did not direct those who engaged in sin to suffer sorrow, but to alter their manner of everyday life, to "produce fruit consistent with repentance."[239] Like faith, repentance remains useless when not accompanied by action.

---

[236] 2 Corinthians 7:9 NASU (New American Standard Bible Update, 1995 revision). For more information about the NASU, see the copyright page, among the first pages of this book.

[237] *Elupéthete* (ĕ-lü-pá-thā-tĕ), ἐλυπήθητέ

[238] *Lupéo* (lü-pĕ́-ō), λυπέω

[239] Matthew 3:8 BT; Luke 3:8; Acts 26:20

Fruit Consistent with Repentance

"Produce fruit consistent with repentance,"[240] John the Immerser scolded the Sadducees and Pharisees.[241] The Pharisees and Sadducees had not come to John intending to change their hypocritical ways. Instead, they planned to acquire praise from the people by making a public display of their immersion[242] in the Jordan River by the desert prophet.

Consider how Jesus portrayed the primary motivation of those hypocritical religious leaders.

- *"So then, when <u>you</u> give alms, do not sound a trumpet in front of you as, indeed, the hypocrites do in the synagogues and in the streets, **so that they might be praised by men**."*[243]

- *"And when <u>you</u>[244] pray, do not be like the hypocrites; because they love to pray standing in the synagogues and on the street corners, **so that they might be noticed by men**."*[245]

- *"When <u>you</u> fast, do not put on a sad face like the hypocrites do. They disfigure their faces while fasting, **so that they might be noticed by men**."*[246]

---

[240] Matthew 3:8 BT; Luke 3:8; Acts 26:20

[241] For information concerning the Pharisee and Sadducee sects of the Jews, see "Glossary."

[242] For a discussion of immersion, see the book *Born to Die* (by Chuck Bagby), "Chapter 8 – The Desert Prophet," heading "They Were Immersed (Matthew 3:6)."

[243] Matthew 6:2 BT

[244] To convey the intent of the Greek text, the BT (Bagby Translation) marks *you* and *your* with a double underscore when plural (i.e., <u>you</u>, <u>your</u>). For additional information regarding the BT's use of the double underscore, see "Appendix 5: Bagby Translation (BT)," subheading "You and Your."

[245] Matthew 6:5 BT

[246] Matthew 6:16 BT

- *"**They do all their works in order to be noticed by people**. For they widen their phylacteries and enlarge their tassels. Also, they love the reclining place of honor at banquets, and the preeminent seats in the synagogues, and the greetings in the markets, and to be called Rabbi by people."*[247]

The Sadducees and Pharisees did gain the attention of the people that day, not through the popular praise they craved, but by way of the public humiliation brought on by John's reprimand, "produce fruit consistent with repentance."[248]

---

[247] Matthew 23:5-7 BT
[248] Matthew 3:8 BT; Luke 3:8; Acts 26:20

Do You Have Faith in God's Promise?

Repentance, a Christian's first work of faith, requires alignment with God's wishes.

To ease our shame, the Creator advised through His prophet Paul,

> *Sorrow that is according to the will of God produces repentance ..., **leading to salvation**.*[249]

Similarly, He entreated through the apostle Peter,

> *Repent and return, so that your **sins may be wiped away**.*[250]

Following careful consideration of consequences, a penitent person launches an altered lifestyle. Self-interest no longer remains primary. Godly thoughts and behavior replace sin as a way of life. The gains pledged by God far outweigh the waste left behind.[251]

You know God's promise. Trust Him to hold to it. Demonstrate faith in Him. Follow through – "produce fruit consistent with repentance.[252]

> *"Repent and turn to God,*
> *performing **deeds appropriate for repentance** "*[253]
> (Paul to King Agrippa)

> *"God is now declaring to men that*
> *all people everywhere should **repent** "*[254]
> (Paul to the Athenians)

---

[249] 2 Corinthians 7:10[a] NASU
[250] Acts 3:19 NASU
[251] Philippians 3:8
[252] Matthew 3:8 BT; Luke 3:8; Acts 26:20
[253] Acts 26: 20 NASU
[254] Acts 17:30 NASU

***

Contemplation Points

1. When John the Immerser and Jesus proclaimed all should "repent," what did they expect of their listeners?

2. How have you produced "fruit consistent with repentance?"[255]

---

[255] Matthew 3:8 BT; Luke 3:8; Acts 26:20

....

CHAPTER 9

Walk by Faith, Not by Sight

> *Therefore, being always of good courage,*
> *and knowing that while we are at home in the body*
> *we are absent from the Lord ... we* **walk**[256] **by faith,**
> **not by sight** ....[257]

(Paul to the Christians in Corinth)

Paul's point? When the Corinthian Christians one day reside in Heaven with the Lord Jesus, they will *see* Him, as well as the fulfillment of His commitments. At that time, they will walk by sight. Until then, while they remain absent from the Lord, while at home in the body on Earth, they must *walk by faith*.

---

[256] In the Scriptures, the word *walk* frequently serves as a metaphorical reference to *lifestyle*, as in 2 Corinthians 5:7.

[257] 2 Corinthians 5:6-7 NASU; For emphasis, the author has placed selected words in bold font within passages of Scripture quoted in this book.

Paul reminded them that through faith they "look not at the things which are seen, but at the things which are not seen; for the things which are seen are temporal, but the things which are not seen are eternal."[258]

> *Faith is the **substantiation** of things being hoped for,*
> *the **conviction** of things not seen.*
> (Hebrews 11:1 BT)[259]

---

[258] 2 Corinthians 4:18 NASU

[259] BT (Bagby Translation) designates a passage of Scripture translated by Dr. Chuck Bagby. For more information regarding the BT, see "Appendix 5: Bagby Translation (BT)."

Not by Sight

By reminding the Corinthian Christians that "we walk by faith, not by sight," Paul implied their faith in God did not require them to see what God has promised. Instead, by examining circumstantial evidence, indirect evidence that logically proves a fact, the Corinthian believers *substantiated* that the Lord Jesus exists as God[260] and will honor His commitments to them.

Having attained fundamental knowledge and analyzed circumstantial evidence, they became convinced that Jesus will deliver what He has pledged. The Corinthian disciples demonstrated their *conviction* through works of faith (trusting actions based on substantiated fact). They walked by faith (knowledge × trust) on Earth until they could walk by sight in Heaven, where they would see their Lord and the fulfillment of His word.

Consistent with God's Definition of Faith

To "walk by faith, not by sight" harmonizes with God's definition of faith found in Hebrews 11:1. While on Earth, unable to see the spiritual realm, we cannot "walk by sight." Instead, we must trust the knowledge we gained through critical thinking.[261] We must "walk by faith."

---

[260] Jesus is God. See Matthew 1:23. [NOTE: *Immanuel* (or *Emmanuel*), an English transliteration of the Greek name *Emmanuál* (ĕm-mä-nü-ál, Ἐμμανουήλ), itself a transliteration of the Hebrew name *Imanuél* (ĭm-ā-nü-él, עִמָּנוּאֵל) which means "God with us."] See also John 1:18; 20:28; Colossians 1:16-17; 2:9; Titus 2:13; and Isaiah 9:6.

[261] Critical thinking occurs when one bases beliefs and behavior on the exercise of careful reasoning founded on sound evidence and intellectual integrity.

FAITH	=	**KNOWLEDGE**	×	**TRUST**
		(Substantiated Fact, Fact-based Belief)		(Conviction, Follow-through, Trusting Action Based on Knowledge)

*Faith is the **substantiation** of things being hoped for,
the **conviction** of things not seen.*
(Hebrews 11:1 BT)

Circumstantial Evidence

Following the example of the Corinthians, we must not limit ourselves to direct observation to determine truth. We do not have to see God to know He exists or that His promises prove credible. Rather, we engage in critical thinking as we investigate the circumstantial evidences that reveal God and *substantiate* our reasons for trusting Him.

Just as the pattern of a fingerprint on glass (a circumstantial evidence) *proves* a specific person touched that object, the layout of the universe, from the smallest subatomic particle to vast galaxies, establishes the existence of an intelligent Designer/Creator. That Creator gave us *His* Scriptures, written by *His* prophets, to substantiate *His* existence, power, love, trustworthiness, and history with mankind.

Paul explained to the Christians in Rome that skeptics who deny the existence of the Creator have compromised their intellectual integrity[262] by disregarding the vast circumstantial evidence of "what has been made."[263] Only by ignoring the indirect evidence that indicates intelligent design of the universe can disbelievers discredit the Designer-Maker. Concerning such scoffers, Paul wrote to the Roman believers,

> *That which is known about God is evident within them: for God made it evident to them. For since the creation of the world His invisible attributes, His eternal power and divine nature, have been clearly seen, **being understood through what has been made**, so that they are without excuse.*[264]

---

[262] Intellectual integrity – To maintain intellectual integrity, one must remain 1) objective, 2) unslanted by preconceptions or biases, 3) free of contradictory beliefs, and 4) without self-deception.

[263] Romans 1:19-20 NASU; See also Isaiah 41:18-20 and Psalm 19:1-2.

[264] Romans 1:19-20 NASU

Tap your intellect. Reason with yourself. The sun exists even when you do not see it. You allow circumstantial evidence to substantiate its presence. With conviction (trusting action) you carry out your activities, knowing it still exists. Similarly, God lives though you do not see Him, "being understood through what has been made."

The apostle[265] Peter comforted distant Christians who, although they had never seen Jesus, knew and trusted Him. Living in regions of the Asian peninsula between the Black Sea and Mediterranean Sea,[266] among cultures of unbelievers, they suffered as they walked by faith. To those devoted Christians, Peter wrote,

> *Though **you have not seen Him** [Jesus],[267] you love Him, and though **you do not see Him** now, but **believe** [have faith in] in Him, you greatly rejoice with joy inexpressible and full of glory, obtaining as the outcome of your faith the salvation of your souls.[268]*

---

[265] Apostle – *transliteration* of the Greek word *apóstolos* (ä-pŏ-stŏ-lŏs), ἀπόστολος, a common Greek word describing any delegate. When *transliterating*, a translator spells out an approximation of the original language's pronunciation of a word, using the alphabet of the second language. Within the Scriptures, "apostles" typically refers to the 12 followers chosen by Jesus to officially represent Him. For lists of the original twelve, see Matthew 10:1-4; Mark 3:13-19; Luke 6:12-16; and Acts 1:13 (which excludes Judas Iscariot, who had died).

[266] 1 Peter 1:1; Pontus, Galatia, Cappadocia, Asia, Bithynia

[267] The author added [Jesus] to clarify the context.

[268] 1 Peter 1:8-9 NASU

Knowledge (Substantiated Fact)

Paul reminded the Corinthian Christians, none of whom had ever seen Jesus, to "walk by faith, not by sight."[269] By exercising critical thinking, they *substantiated* the information Paul taught them and thus obtained essential *knowledge* of Jesus and His assurances. Based on the knowledge they gained, they chose a lifestyle of trusting actions (conviction, works of faith, follow-through).

Trust (Conviction)

Like us, the Corinthian disciples had no opportunity to directly observe Jesus. Consequently, they exercised critical thinking to gain the knowledge (substantiated fact) on which to establish their faith. Having *substantiated* the crucial details, they then had reason to proceed with a life of *conviction* (trusting actions, works of faith, follow-through). They "walked by faith," trusting the Lord they had come to know.

A time will come when Christians who have totally submitted to God will see the Lord and live amid His fulfilled promises. Until then, they "walk by faith, not by sight."

---

[269] 2 Corinthians 5:7 NASU

***

Contemplation Points

1. Do you exercise critical thinking[270] to establish your faith?

    a. If so, explain how.

    b. If not, explain why not.

2. Write the first sentence of your reply to a skeptic who insists, "Seeing is believing." (That is, he will not believe Jesus exists or exercised supernatural power unless he observes it himself.)

---

[270] Critical thinking occurs when one bases beliefs and behavior on the exercise of careful reasoning founded on sound evidence and intellectual integrity.

CHAPTER 10

....

Blind Faith vs. God-Defined Faith

When Paul pointed out, "we walk by faith, not by sight,"[271] he did not suggest God wants His people to disregard knowledge (substantiated fact) as the basis for their faith. God doesn't desire that we mindlessly trust Him to keep His word. Never has He urged anyone to maintain a *blind faith*.[272]

How long ago mankind devised the term *blind faith* and first employed it within one of its diverse religious theologies[273] remains uncertain. Yet, that God did not originate the phrase stands sure, for it never occurs in His Scriptures. Nonetheless, God does recognize the ravaging effects religious blindness wreaks on spiritual health.

---

[271] 2 Corinthians 5:7 NASU

[272] Blind Faith – Our culture typically portrays *blind faith* as a trust that lacks reason, an illogical belief.

[273]Theology, when referred to in this work, consists of any human-crafted system of religious interpretations, traditions, creeds, opinions, legends, myths, or combination of these items compiled or promoted by a religious leader, sect, denomination, or organization.

God's View of Blindness

Although God's prophets never employed the phrase *blind faith* in the Scriptures, God has never closed His eyes to the harsh consequences of blindness, whether physical blindness or spiritual blindness. Consider the following passages in which Jesus, Peter, and Paul utilized the words "blind" or "see" figuratively as they addressed spiritual health.

Jesus to His Apostles

Then, approaching Him [Jesus],[274] *the disciples*[275] [Jesus' apostles] *said, "Are You aware that the **Pharisees** were offended when they heard that statement?"*

*Then, answering, He said, "Every plant that My heavenly Father has not planted will be uprooted. Let them be. They are **blind guides of the blind**. And, if a **blind person guides the blind, both will fall** into a ditch."*[276]

Jesus to His Apostles

Afterward, having come up to Him [Jesus], *the disciples* [Jesus' apostles] *said, "Why do You speak to them in parables?"*

Then, answering, He said to them, "Because, to <u>you</u> [Jesus' apostles] *it has been granted to know the mysteries of the Kingdom of the Heavens. However, to them, it has not been given. ... That is why I speak to them with parables; because, **while seeing, they do not see**, and while hearing, they do not hear, nor do they **understand**.*[277]

---

[274] The author inserted [Jesus] to clarify the context.

[275] The term *disciple* means "learner" and refers to believers who follow the teachings of Jesus. In the Scriptures, sometimes the word describes those who followed John the Immerser's teachings (Matthew 9:14). At other times, the context in which a writer employed the word indicates a reference specifically to Jesus' apostles, as in Matthew 15:12-14.

[276] Matthew 15:12-14 BT

[277] Matthew 13:10-13 BT

Jesus to Pharisees and Their Scribes

*Woe to <u>you</u>, **scribes and Pharisees, hypocrites**, because <u>you</u> tithe mint and anise and cumin, yet <u>you</u> neglect the weightier matters of the Law – justice and mercy and faith. Now, it is necessary to practice these things without neglecting the others.*

***Blind guides**, those who filter out a gnat while gulping down a camel.*

***Woe** to <u>you</u>, **scribes and Pharisees, hypocrites**, because <u>you</u> clean the outside of the cup and the dish, but inside they are full of extortion and self-indulgence.*

***Blind** Pharisee, first clean the inside of the cup, so that the outside of it may also become clean.*

***Woe** to <u>you</u>, **scribes and Pharisees, hypocrites**, because <u>you</u> are like whitewashed tombs, which on the outside appear to be truly beautiful, but inside they are full of bones of the dead and all uncleanness. In the same way, on the outside, <u>you</u>, too, appear to people to be truly righteous, but inside <u>you</u> are full of **hypocrisy and lawlessness**.*[278]

---

[278] Matthew 23:23-28 BT

Paul to Corinthian Christians

*And even if our gospel is veiled, it is veiled to those who are perishing, in whose case the god of this world has **blinded the minds** of the unbelieving so that they might **not see**[279] **the light of the gospel** of the glory of Christ, who is the image of God.*[280]

Peter to Christians in General

*Now for this very reason also, applying all diligence, **in your faith supply** moral excellence, and in your moral excellence, **knowledge**, and in your knowledge, self-control, and in your self-control, perseverance, and in your perseverance, godliness, and in your godliness, brotherly kindness, and in your brotherly kindness, love.*

*For if these qualities are yours and are increasing, they render you neither useless nor unfruitful in the **true knowledge** of our Lord Jesus Christ.*

*For **he who lacks these qualities is blind** or short-sighted, ...*[281]

---

[279] In this passage, Paul used the word "see" figuratively, meaning "know, understand."

[280] 2 Corinthians 4:3-4 NASU

[281] 2 Peter 1:5-9 NASU

Blind Faith in Blind Guides

Jesus employed the concept of unknowing, unseeing, *blind* faith when He addressed the Jewish religious leaders who pursued Him, who shadowed His every move and plotted how to trap Him in His reasoning.[282]

"Woe to <u>you</u>,[283] **blind guides**," Jesus scolded the Pharisees[284] and their scribes.[285]

Those spiritually sightless religious leaders boldly declared to Jesus, "We have one Father: God."[286]

Jesus countered, "You **know** neither Me nor My Father, … It is My Father who glorifies Me, of whom you say, 'He is our God'; and you have **not come to know Him**."[287]

Speaking of the undiscerning, blind faith possessed by many Jews, Jesus explained to His followers, "While seeing, **they do not see**[288] … **nor do they understand**."[289] "They are **blind guides** of the **blind**. And, if a **blind** person **guides the blind, both will fall** into a ditch."[290]

Those spiritually blind Jewish leaders *claimed* God as their Father, yet had "not come to **know** Him."[291] Though well acquainted

---

[282] Matthew 22:15,18; Mark 12:13; Luke 11:53-54

[283] To convey the intent of the Greek text, the BT (Bagby Translation) marks *you* and *your* with a double underscore when plural (i.e., <u>you</u>, <u>your</u>). For additional information regarding the BT's use of the double underscore, see "Appendix 5: Bagby Translation (BT)," subheading "You and Your."

[284] Pharisees – For information concerning the Pharisee sect of the Jews, see "Glossary."

[285] For information regarding scribes, see "Glossary."

[286] John 8:41 NASU

[287] John 8:19,54-55 NASU

[288] In this passage, Jesus used the word "see" figuratively, meaning "know, understand."

[289] Matthew 13:13 BT

[290] Matthew 15:12-14 BT

[291] John 8:55 NASU

with the Scriptures, they failed to recognize God's message. They chose to replace His directives with the traditional, man-made *interpretations* of their religious sect.[292] They perverted their intellectual integrity, twisting selected segments of Scripture in vain attempts to rationalize their theology.[293] They preferred to ignore passages that would expose their unsound teachings.

Zeal Without Knowledge

Jesus' apostle Paul commented concerning those spiritually unsighted Jewish religious leaders, writing,

> *I testify about them that they have a zeal for God, but not in accordance with **knowledge**.*[294]

Those religious guides had passion for God, yet challenged Jesus because their spiritual fervor lacked true knowledge.

God's definition of faith in Hebrews 11:1 identified substantiated fact (knowledge) as one of the two indispensable requisites of the faith He requires His people to possess. *Blind* faith, unknowing faith, does not fulfill God's expectation of us.

FAITH	=	KNOWLEDGE	×	TRUST
		(Substantiated Fact, Fact-based Belief)		(Conviction, Works of Faith, Trusting Action Based on Knowledge, Follow-through)

---

[292] Matthew 15:1-9; Mark 7:1-13

[293] Theology, when referred to in this work, consists of any human-crafted system of religious interpretations, traditions, creeds, opinions, legends, myths, or combination of these items compiled or promoted by a religious leader, sect, denomination, or organization.

[294] Romans 10:2 NASU

False Knowledge

Blind faith lacks an authentic knowledge base. In contrast, the faith God demands of His people requires genuine knowledge (substantiated fact), coupled with trusting action (conviction, works of faith, follow-through). God does not want Christians to base their lifestyle (walk) on the teachings of spiritually blind guides who deprive their followers of true spiritual knowledge.

Desperation, susceptibility to social pressure, and lack of critical thinking predispose some to trust spiritually blind religious leaders who teach error. Sidestepping godly reason, those misguided individuals invest their lives in subjective[295] self-delusion, legend, myth, and superstition, trusting counterfeit knowledge.[296] They do not possess faith as God defined it in Hebrews 11:1.

> *Faith is the **substantiation** of things being hoped for,*
> *the **conviction** of things not seen.*
> (Hebrews 11:1 BT)

Paul would likely counsel such misinformed, spiritually immature people with the same words he wrote to the Christians in the city of Ephesus.

> *We are no longer to be children, tossed here and there by waves and carried about by every wind of doctrine, by the trickery of men, by craftiness in deceitful scheming; but ... **we are to grow up** ....*[297]

---

[295] Subjective – based on feelings rather than logic
[296] Colossians 2:20-23
[297] Ephesians 4:14-15 NASU

Blind Faith »→ Oxymoron

Jesus wants us to have *seeing* faith based on true knowledge. He cringes at *blind* faith founded on the teachings of religious leaders who corrupt their intellectual integrity by wrenching the Scriptures to conform to their theology.

When someone declares that they exercise *blind faith*, that assertion contains an oxymoron.[298] Jesus clarified that spiritual blindness indicates an absence of true spiritual knowledge. Yet, God's definition of faith demands that His people possess knowledge (substantiated fact) in order to attain the faith He desires them to realize. *Blind* faith leads a person to "fall into a ditch"[299] – spiritual self-destruction. The concept of blindness does not harmonize with God's definition of faith.

Woe to you lawyers [scribes]*![300]*
*For you have taken away the **key of knowledge** ....[301]*
(Jesus to the Jewish Scribes)

FAITH	=	KNOWLEDGE	×	TRUST
		(Substantiated Fact, Fact-based Belief)		(Conviction, Works of Faith, Trusting Action Based on Knowledge, Follow-through)

---

[298] Oxymoron – a two-word phrase containing terms defined by contradictory meanings. Examples include cruel kindness, deafening silence, exact estimate, genuine imitation, and blind faith.

[299] Matt 15:14 BT

[300] The author added [scribes] to clarify the context. The term "lawyers" referred to scribes. For additional information regarding scribes, see "Glossary."

[301] Luke 11:52 NASU

*Faith is the **substantiation** of things being hoped for,
the **conviction** of things not seen.*
(Hebrews 11:1 BT)

Beware of anyone who urges you to pursue *blind* faith.

***

Contemplation Points

1. Who would Jesus identify as "blind guides" today?

2. Paul explained to the Roman Christians that the Jewish religious leaders, those Jesus referred to as *blind guides*, "have a zeal for God, but not "in accordance with knowledge." (Romans 10:2 NASU)

   a. How do you ensure you do not base your faith on the teachings of "blind guides?"

   b. How do you make certain your zeal for God remains in accordance with knowledge (i.e., substantiated fact)?

CHAPTER 11

....

Saving Faith

*Continue in the things you have **learned** and
become **convinced of**, knowing from whom you have learned them,
and that from childhood you have **known** the **sacred writings**
which are able to give you the **wisdom** that
leads to salvation through faith
which is in Christ Jesus.* [302]
(The apostle Paul to the evangelist Timothy)

As a youth, Timothy *learned* the Scriptures from his mother Eunice and grandmother Lois. [303] By exercising critical thinking, he substantiated the points taught him and thus became *convinced of* what he had learned. Consequently, he acquired *wisdom* through his knowledge of the *sacred writings*. That wisdom, gained from his knowledge of the Scriptures, led him to *salvation through faith*.

---

[302] 2 Timothy 3:14-15 NASU
[303] 2 Timothy 1:5

Note the process explained by Paul that steered Timothy to salvation.

1. *Learned* the Scriptures

2. Became *convinced of* (substantiated) what he had learned (i.e., gained knowledge)

3. Gleaned *wisdom* due to his knowledge of the Scriptures

4. Found *salvation through faith* (because of the wisdom he gained from the Scriptures)

Timothy possessed the saving faith God desires everyone to attain.

> *Faith is the **substantiation** of things being hoped for,*
> *the **conviction** of things not seen.*
> (Hebrews 11:1 BT)

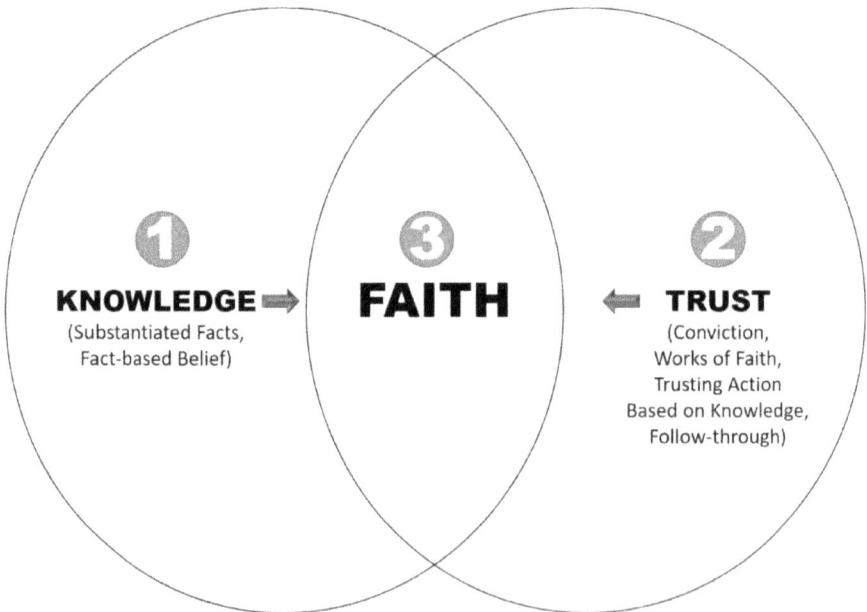

① KNOWLEDGE ➡
(Substantiated Facts,
Fact-based Belief)

③ FAITH

⬅ **② TRUST**
(Conviction,
Works of Faith,
Trusting Action
Based on Knowledge,
Follow-through)

***

Contemplation Point

Timothy substantiated (i.e., "became convinced of") what Eunice and Lois had taught him.

- How did you substantiate (become convinced of) the validity or invalidity of what others taught you?

    o Provide an example.

What About the Gift of God? (Ephesians 2:8-9)

*For by grace you have been **saved** through faith;*
*and that not of yourselves, it is the **gift** of God;*
not as a result of works, so that no one may boast.[304]

When Paul wrote of saving faith to the Ephesian Christians, he did not insinuate that God infuses a person with faith as a gift, but that by His grace, He gives *salvation* to those who demonstrate faith. Through faith a believer becomes "justified as a gift by His grace."[305]

Nobody earns salvation. God allows faith to save only because He extends His *grace* (unmerited benevolence) to a person who exhibits conviction (works of faith, trusting action based on knowledge, follow-through). Remember, Paul told the Ephesians, "by grace you have been saved *through* faith."

God grants His gift of salvation graciously, but conditionally. Only a person who has displayed faith becomes a beneficiary of the free "gift of God" to which Paul referred in Ephesians 2:8. Even the thief crucified on a cross next to Jesus possessed *faith* in Jesus. He possessed *knowledge*, for he spoke of Jesus' innocence and His coming kingdom. Together with this, he demonstrated *trust* (conviction) that Jesus' life and power would continue following crucifixion when he said to Him, "Jesus, remember me when you come in Your kingdom."[306]

By His grace, God saves a person through faith once that individual has established faith.[307] "By *grace* you have been saved,"[308] Paul explained to the Christians in Ephesus. Likewise,

---

[304] Ephesians 2:8-9 NASU
[305] Romans 3:24 NASU
[306] Luke 23:42 NASU
[307] Remember God's definition of saving faith found in Hebrews 11:1. Faith = substantiation × conviction = knowledge × trust.
[308] Ephesians 2:5 NASU

Peter reminded the brethren in Jerusalem, "we are saved through the *grace* of our Lord Jesus."[309]

God's grace supplies the authority behind saving faith. A Christian's faith saves only because God permits it, by His grace (unmerited benevolence). Salvation through faith cannot exist without God's grace.

What About the Spiritual Gift?
(1 Corinthians 12:9)

In the 12th chapter of 1st Corinthians, Paul transitioned his readers into the context[310] of spiritual gifts. He wrote this letter to Christians in Corinth, people who had previously devoted their lives to Jesus. Jesus, in turn, had forgiven their sins. He saved them *before* Paul wrote his 1st Corinthian letter.

Note, Paul addressed the topic of spiritual gifts in 1 Corinthians 12:1-10. He did not discuss *saving* faith. Keep in mind, Jesus had *already* saved those believers!

Paul wrote to them,

> *Now concerning spiritual gifts, brethren, I do not want you to be unaware. ... Now there are varieties of gifts, but the same Spirit. ... For* **to one** *is given the word of wisdom through the Spirit, and* **to another** *the word of knowledge according to the same Spirit;* **to another faith** *by the same Spirit, and* **to another** *gifts of healing by the one Spirit, and* **to another** *the effecting of miracles, and* **to another** *prophecy, and to another the distinguishing of spirits,* **to another** *various kinds of tongues, and* **to another** *the interpretation of tongues.*[311]

---

[309] Acts 15:11 NASU

[310] Context, the communication before and after a word or passage, often sheds light on the meaning intended by the writer or speaker.

[311] 1 Corinthians 12:1-10 NASU

In Paul's remarks quoted above, the repeated phrase *to another* proves significant. Note that the Corinthian disciples did not receive identical gifts. Any one of them might have received

1. "The word of wisdom through the Spirit," or
2. "The word of knowledge by the same Spirit," or
3. "**Faith** by the same Spirit," or
4. "Gifts of healing by the one Spirit," or
5. "The effecting of miracles," or
6. "Prophecy," or
7. "The distinguishing of spirits," or
8. "Various kinds of tongues," or
9. "The interpretation of tongues."

Don't skip over Paul's point number 3! He truly wrote, "*to another faith* by the same Spirit." Those Corinthian Christians already possessed *saving* faith. Paul explained that some (not everybody) also received the *spiritual gift* of faith.[312]

The spiritual gift of faith went beyond the saving faith Paul mentioned to the Christians of Ephesus when he wrote, "for by grace you have been saved through faith."[313] Nor did it equate to the saving faith mentioned in Hebrews 11:6, "without faith it is impossible to please Him."[314] Not explained in detail by God in His Scriptures,[315] the spiritual gift of faith in some way supplemented saving faith.

---

[312] 1 Corinthians 12:9

[313] Ephesians 2:8 NASU

[314] Hebrews 11:6 NASU

[315] We must remain content with Moses' statement to Israel, "The secret things belong to the Lord our God, but the things revealed belong to us and to our sons forever ..." (Deuteronomy 29:29 NASU).

What About the Measure of Faith?
(Romans 12:3)

As in 1 Corinthians 12:9, Paul does *not* address the topic of saving faith in Romans chapter 12. Jesus had already saved those Roman Christians. Paul focused on the context of *humility* in Romans 12:3-8.

He wrote to the brethren in Rome,

*For through the grace given to me I say to everyone among you not to think more highly of himself than he ought to think; but to think so as to have sound judgment, as God has allotted to each a **measure of faith**. For just as we have many members in one body and all the members do not have the same function, so we, who are many, are one body in Christ, and individually members one of another. Since we have **gifts that differ** according to the grace given to us, each of us is to exercise them accordingly: if prophecy, according to the **proportion of his faith**; if service, in his serving; or he who teaches, in his teaching; or he who exhorts, in his exhortation; he who gives, with liberality; he who leads, with diligence; he who shows mercy, with cheerfulness.* [316]

After writing, "God has allotted to each a *measure* of faith," Paul followed with, "we have gifts that differ" and "if prophecy, according to the *proportion* of his faith." The term "measure of faith," correlates directly with "proportion of his faith." Just as those spiritual gifts differed, such as prophecy, service, teaching, exhortation, giving, leading, and showing mercy, so did the measure/proportion of faith God assigned to facilitate the implementation of each gift.

Keep in mind, those Roman Christians already possessed saving faith. That measure/proportion of faith Paul mentioned in the

---

[316] Romans 12:3-8 NASU

12th chapter of his letter to the Roman believers went beyond the saving faith mentioned in Hebrews 11:6, "without faith it is impossible to please Him."[317] Neither did it correspond to the saving faith Paul discussed with the Ephesian disciples when he wrote, "for by grace you have been saved through faith."[318] Nor did it duplicate the spiritual gift of faith Paul mentioned in 1 Corinthians 12:9. The measure/proportion of faith mentioned by Paul in Romans 12, not explained in detail by God in His Scriptures,[319] in some way enabled a disciple who had received a spiritual gift to exercise it effectively.[320]

Paul cautioned each Roman disciple not to think himself more important than another disciple who had not received the same spiritual gift. Each Christian's role complements that of the others.

He explained,

> *For the body is not one member, but many. If the foot says, "Because I am not a hand, I am not a part of the body," it is not for this reason any the less a part of the body. And if the ear says, "Because I am not an eye, I am not a part of the body," it is not for this reason any the less a part of the body.*
>
> *If the whole body were an eye, where would the hearing be? If the whole were hearing, where would the sense of smell be? But now God has placed the members, each one*

---

[317] Hebrews 11:6 NASU

[318] Ephesians 2:8 NASU

[319] God does not disclose all details about everything, as with the *spiritual gift of faith* Paul mentioned in 1 Corinthians 12:1,9 and the *measure/proportion* of faith he wrote of in Romans 12:3,6. We must remain content with Moses' statement to Israel, "The secret things belong to the Lord our God, but the things revealed belong to us and to our sons forever ..." (Deuteronomy 29:29 NASU).

[320] Continue open to the possibility that neither the *spiritual gift of faith*, nor the *measure/proportion* of faith, had application for later generations of Christians, and for this reason God did not have His prophets discuss its nature in their writings for us. In contrast, *saving* faith relates to all generations, hence God had His prophets discuss it in detail.

of them, in the body, just as He desired.

If they were all one member, where would the body be? But now there are many members, but one body. And the eye cannot say to the hand, "I have no need of you"; or again the head to the feet, "I have no need of you."

On the contrary, it is much truer that the members of the body which seem to be weaker are necessary; and those members of the body which we deem less honorable, on these we bestow more abundant honor, and our less presentable members become much more presentable, whereas our more presentable members have no need of it.

But God has so composed the body, giving more abundant honor to that member which lacked, so that there may be no division in the body, but that the members may have the same care for one another. And if one member suffers, all the members suffer with it; if one member is honored, all the members rejoice with it.

Now you are Christ's body, and individually members of it.[321]

---

[321] 1 Corinthians 12:14-27 NASU

CHAPTER 12

···

Deceitful or Trustful Feelings?

"Listen to your heart."

"Trust your heart."

"Follow your heart."

The three lines above contain advice many hear when making a life-defining decision. That well-wishing counsel amounts to *trust your feelings*.

Warnings from God

God cautioned those who would trust their feelings (trust their heart). His warnings include the following.

- *The heart is more deceitful than all else ....*[322]

- *He who trusts in his own heart is a fool,*
  But he who walks wisely will be delivered.[323]

- *Follow the impulses of your heart and ... know that God will bring you to judgment for all these things.*[324]

---

[322] Jeremiah 17:9 NASU
[323] Proverbs 28:26 NASU
[324] Ecclesiastes 11:9 NASU

Contexts of "Heart"

To understand how the *heart* relates to the nature of the saving faith God intends His people to acquire, one must first identify the context in which a prophet used *heart* in any given passage. God's prophets often utilized *heart* within contexts other than that of feelings. They employed *heart* in four distinct contexts, the literal anatomical (body part), as well as three metaphorical[325] contexts – depth, feelings, and mind.

1. Anatomical (Body Part)

A sampling of *heart* passages written within the literal anatomical context includes the following.

- *Then Joab said, "I will not waste time here with you." So he took **three spears** in his hand and **thrust them through the heart of Absalom** while he was yet alive in the midst of the oak.*[326]

- *And Jehu drew his bow with his full strength and shot Joram between his arms; and the **arrow went through his heart** and he sank in his chariot.*[327]

- *Their **sword will enter their own heart**, and their bows will be broken.*[328]

- *My **heart throbs**, my strength fails me; And the light of my eyes, even that has gone from me.*[329]

---

[325] A metaphor, a figure of speech, describes a characteristic or action of one noun (person, place, or thing) by replacing it in a sentence with a second *dissimilar* noun, suggesting a similarity between the two nouns. For more information about metaphors, see "Glossary."

[326] 2 Samuel 18:14 NASU

[327] 2 Kings 9:24 NASU

[328] Psalm 37:15 NASU

[329] Psalm 38:10 NASU

2. Depth/Distance (into a Sea, the Earth, etc.)

A sampling of *heart* passages written within the metaphorical depth/distance context includes the following.

- *Therefore we will not fear, though the earth should change and though the mountains slip into the **heart of the sea** ....*[330]

- *The ships of Tarshish were the carriers for your merchandise. And you were filled and were very glorious in the **heart of the seas**. Your rowers have brought you into great waters; the east wind has broken you in the **heart of the seas**. Your wealth, your wares, your merchandise, your sailors and your pilots, your repairers of seams, your dealers in merchandise and all your men of war who are in you, with all your company that is in your midst, will fall into the **heart of the seas** on the day of your overthrow.*[331]

- *Son of man, say to the leader of Tyre, 'Thus says the Lord God, "Because your heart is lifted up and you have said, 'I am a god, I sit in the seat of gods in the **heart of the seas**' ....*[332]

- *For just as Jonah was three days and three nights in the belly of the sea monster, so will the Son of Man be three days and three nights in the **heart of the earth**.*[333]

---

[330] Psalm 46:2 NASU
[331] Ezekiel 27:25-27 NASU
[332] Ezekiel 28:2 NASU
[333] Matthew 12:40 NASU

3. Feelings (Emotions, Sentiments)

Another metaphorical context of *heart* within Scripture concerns a person's *feelings*, including joy, gladness, merriment, exultation, happiness, delight, cheerfulness, sadness, sorrow, anguish, fear, terror, pride, arrogance, haughtiness, hatefulness, anxiety, humility, etc. A sampling of *heart* passages written within the feelings context includes the following.

- *So the king said to me, "Why is your face sad though you are not sick? This is nothing but **sadness** of **heart**." Then I was very much afraid.*[334]

- *When my **heart** was **embittered** and I was pierced within ....*[335]

- *A **joyful heart** makes a cheerful face, but when the **heart** is **sad**, the spirit is broken.*[336]

- *Say to those with **anxious heart**, "Take courage, fear not. Behold, your God will come with vengeance; the recompense of God will come, but He will save you.*[337]

- *I have great **sorrow** and unceasing **grief** in my **heart** ....*[338]

---

[334] Nehemiah 2:2 NASU
[335] Psalm 73:21 NASU
[336] Proverbs 15:13 NASU
[337] Isaiah 35:4 NASU
[338] Romans 9:2 NASU

Deceitful Heart/Feelings

Deceitful feelings, sentiments that lack a factual foundation, lead a person to believe and act on untruths. Beware! Satan turns human emotional fascination into a devious spiritual weapon.

For example, concerning the fruit tree from which God forbade Adam and Eve to eat, Satan fooled Eve into trusting her *feelings*. She mistakenly felt "that the tree was *good* for food, and that it was a *delight* to the eyes, and that the tree was *desirable* to make one wise."[339]

Again, hoping to exploit human emotional weakness, Satan took Jesus to the pinnacle of the Temple. Attempting to appeal to His ego, Satan referred to Scripture out of context and taunted,

> *Since[340] You are the Son of God, throw Yourself down. For it has been written that, 'He will command His angels concerning You,'[341] and 'They will lift You up on their hands that Your foot might not stumble over a stone.'[342] [343]*

Applying Scripture within proper context, Jesus responded with spiritual knowledge.

> *It also has been written, 'You shall not test the Lord your God.'[344] [345]*

---

[339] Genesis 3:6 NASU

[340] Since – The Greek word *ei* (ĕĭ, εἰ) can translate as "since" or "if," depending on the context. Here, either translation functions well.

[341] A reference to Psalm 91:11

[342] A reference to Psalm 91:12

[343] Matthew 4:6 BT

[344] A reference to Deuteronomy 6:16

[345] Matthew 4:7 BT

Never allow deceitful feelings of the heart to lead your spiritual life, beliefs, or behavior. When tempted to do so, recall lessons of Scripture as Jesus did, applying them within correct context. Overcome deceitful feelings of the heart with spiritual knowledge.

4. Mind (Intellect)

Still another metaphorical context in which writers utilized *heart* within Scripture addresses human intellect – a *mind* that thinks, ponders, reasons, discerns, understands, knows, etc. A sampling of *heart* passages written within the mind/intellect context includes the following.

- *Let the words of my mouth and the **meditation of my heart** be acceptable in Your sight ….*[346]

- *A **plan in the heart** of a man is like deep water ….*[347]

- *Otherwise they might see with their eyes, hear with their ears, **understand with their hearts**" ….*[348]

- *But Jesus, aware of their reasonings, answered and said to them, "Why are you **reasoning in your hearts**?"*[349]

- *But he who stands firm in his heart, ... being under no constraint, but has **decided** this **in his** own **heart** ….*[350]

- *Each one must do just as he has **purposed in his heart**, not grudgingly or under compulsion ….*[351]

- *For the word of God is living and active and sharper than any two-edged sword, and piercing as far as the division of soul and spirit, of both joints and marrow, and able to judge the **thoughts and intentions of the heart**.*[352]

---

[346] Psalm 19:14 NASU
[347] Proverbs 20:5 NASU
[348] Isaiah 6:10 NASU
[349] Luke 5:22 NASU
[350] 1 Corinthians 7:37 NASU
[351] 2 Corinthians 9:7 NASU
[352] Hebrews 4:12 NASU

Believing with the Heart/Mind

The apostle Paul reminded the Roman Christians that, "With the **heart** a person **believes**."[353] Paul's use of *heart* in the context of *belief* within that passage proves critical when attempting to understand the authentic nature of the saving faith God intends His people to acquire.

One discovers a truth in which to believe through exercise of the mind, not through experiencing an emotion. Hence, when Paul told the disciples in Rome that a person believes with the *heart*, he used *heart* as a metaphor for *mind*.

Belief, Trust, and Faith

The Greek word *pisteúetai* (pĭs-tĕ́ṵ-ĕ-täï),[354] rendered "believes" in Romans 10:10 by the New American Standard Bible Update (NASU), forms the third person singular present passive indicative of the infinitive *pisteúo* (pĭs-tĕ́ṵ-ō)[355] *Pisteúo* means "to believe (a fact), to trust, to faith (i.e., to have faith)." In our language we write "to believe," "to trust," or "to have faith" with distinctive words. However, the Greek[356] language, in which Paul wrote to the Romans Christians, combines those three thoughts into one word – *pisteúo.* Through his statement "with the heart a person believes," Paul effectually communicated, *with the **mind** a person believes/trusts/faiths*.

---

[353] Romans 10:10 NASU

[354] *Pisteúetai* (pĭs-tĕ́ṵ-ĕ-täï, πιστεύεται)

[355] *Pisteúo* (pĭs-tĕ́ṵ-ō, πιστεύω)

[356] The authors of the New Testament books and correspondence wrote their works in Greek, which served as an international language during the first century A.D. due to the enduring Hellenistic (Greek) influence of Alexander the Great's vast conquests three centuries earlier as he expanded his Macedonian Empire. By writing in Greek, New Testament authors effectively communicated within the Roman-Empire, as well as non-Roman Mediterranean cultures.

God Communicates Through One's Mind/Intellect

Throughout history, God consistently revealed information to mankind utilizing human intellectual capacity, employing a person's vocabulary to communicate His messages.[357]

Likewise, when God imparted messages through dreams or visions, He channeled their explanation through an individual's mind, employing human vocabulary.[358]

Similarly, Paul stressed intellect when he wrote to the Roman Christians, "do not be conformed to this world, but be transformed by the renewing of your ***mind***, so that you may prove what the will of God is."[359]

Furthermore, God presented a *logical* case for the Judahites to return to Him and live faithfully, saying, "Let us *reason* together."[360]

But, what about feelings? Doesn't God *speak* to us all by injecting emotions, sentiments, and sensations within us?

God Does Not Deliver Messages via Feelings

Never within His Scriptures did God transmit a message of direction to a human by stimulating sentiments of the heart. Nor did He give reason for anyone to expect Him to do so. He counseled no one to consider "sort of a feeling" an indication of His guidance. To the contrary, He warned,

The heart is more deceitful than all else ....[361]

---

[357] For a few examples of God communicating through human language, see Proverbs 16:1; Genesis 40:1-15; Daniel 4:28-32; and Luke 1:11-20.

[358] Matthew 1:20-21; 1 Kings 3.5-14, For a few examples of God channeling the explanation of a dream through an individual's mind and language, see Daniel 2:1-45; 4:4-27; and Genesis 41:1-36.)

[359] Romans 12:2 NASU

[360] Isaiah 1:18 NASU

[361] Jeremiah 17:9 NASU

Feelings Don't Confirm Salvation

At no time has God suggested sensations confirm saving faith. To the contrary, He specified that *conviction* (trusting action, works of faith, follow-through) based on *substantiation* (what one has reasoned and come to know as fact) form the faith that results in spiritual deliverance.

Yet, some erringly prefer to base their faith on their feelings rather than substantiation and conviction. Take special note that God did not include feelings (emotions, sentiments, sensations) as a factor in *His* definition of faith.

Who dares to modify God's definition?[362] Will you reject His view of faith for the sake of supporting a flawed, traditional, human perspective?[363]

*Faith is the **substantiation** of things being hoped for,*
*the **conviction** of things not seen.*
(Hebrews 11:1 BT)[364]

FAITH	≠	FEELINGS	×	TRUST
		(Emotions, Sentiments, Sensations)		(Trust in One's Feelings)

FAITH	=	KNOWLEDGE	×	TRUST
		(Substantiated Fact, Fact-based Belief)		(Conviction, Works of Faith, Trusting Action Based on Knowledge, Follow-through)

---

[362] See "Chapter 3 – Faith Defined by God."

[363] Colossians 2:8; Matthew 15:3-6; Mark 7:5-9,13

[364] BT (Bagby Translation) designates a passage of Scripture translated by Dr. Chuck Bagby. For more information regarding the BT, see "Appendix 5: Bagby Translation (BT)."

What About Godly Sorrow?

Paul reveals that the Corinthian Christians experienced godly sorrow which led them to repentance.[365] So, doesn't the *feeling* of godly sorrow have something to do with faith? Let's examine how godly sorrow relates to faith.

Jesus' apostle Paul wrote a stern letter to the Christians in Corinth. Members of that congregation had allowed themselves to fall into spiritual disrepair. He scolded them for the following misdeeds, among others.

- Division – They quarreled and divided along man-made brands of Christianity.[366]

- Spiritual immaturity – They had never matured beyond childlike faith.[367]

- Bitterness – A number of the disciples resented any fellow believer who did not align with their preferred brand of Christianity.[368]

- Arrogance[369]

- Sexual immorality – They tolerated among their congregation those involved in forbidden sexual relations.[370]

- Suing one another – They took each other to civil court.[371]

---

[365] 2 Corinthians 7:8-11

[366] 1 Corinthians 1:12-13

[367] 1 Corinthians 3:1-2; 14:20; See "Chapter 8: Childlike Faith" for a discussion of infantile faith.

[368] 1 Corinthians 3:3-9

[369] 1 Corinthians 4:18-19

[370] 1 Corinthians 5:1,9-13; 6:15-18

[371] 1 Corinthians 6:1-10

Godly Sorrow – Opposite of a Deceitful Feeling

Knowledge that they had failed God led the Corinthian Christians to grieve their sinful condition. That information generated a *truthful* feeling within the Corinthian disciples, not a *deceitful* feeling.

Godly sorrow, the reverse of a deceitful feeling, bases itself on fact, making it a *truthful* feeling. In contrast, a *deceitful* feeling lacks a factual foundation and leads an individual to believe and act on untruth, while erroneously convinced they have acted correctly.

The Corinthian brethren based their godly sorrow on the truth that they had come to lead sinful lives. That *knowledge* (substantiation) led them to repent,[372] to demonstrate *trusting action* (conviction) by changing their way of life. A deceitful feeling would have led them to believe and act on an untruth, to deny they had done anything wrong and continue to live outside God's desire.

The Corinthian believers felt godly sorrow, a trustworthy feeling that led them to change their sinful ways. In a follow-up letter, Paul wrote the following to them.

> *I now rejoice, not that you were made sorrowful, but that you were made sorrowful to the point of repentance; for you were made sorrowful according to the will of God .... For the sorrow that is according to the will of God produces a repentance without regret, leading to salvation ....*
> *For behold what earnestness this very thing, this **godly sorrow**, has produced in you: what vindication of yourselves, what indignation, what fear, what longing, what zeal, what avenging of wrong! ....*[373]

---

[372] See "Chapter 8 – Repentance: A Christian's First Work of Faith."
[373] 2 Corinthians 7:8-11 NASU

Heed God's Warnings: Overcome Deceitful Feelings

Your attempts to distinguish between deceitful and truthful feelings may prove challenging. Nonetheless, you must discipline yourself not to permit deceitful feelings, those feelings not generated by spiritual knowledge,[374] to influence your beliefs and actions.

Take care. Deceitful feelings effectively mislead and ensnare. They convince you to believe false truths and do wrong, while *feeling* you have done right.

Heed God's warnings.

- *The heart is more deceitful than all else ....*[375]

- *He who trusts in his own heart is a fool,*
  But he who walks wisely will be delivered.[376]

- *Follow the impulses of your heart and ... know that God*
  will bring you to judgment for all these things.[377]

***

Contemplation Points

1. Do you trust God to fulfill the promises He made to you through His Scriptures?

    a. If so, why?

    b. If not, why not?

2. Do you trust your feelings more than God's Scriptures?

    a. If so, why?

    b. If not, why not?

---

[374] Knowledge (substantiated fact) serves as one of the factors used by God to define faith in Hebrews 11:1. All of mankind's spiritual knowledge comes from God (Proverbs 2:6; Psalm 119:66,169; 2 Timothy 3:16-17; 2 Peter 1:20-21). A few passages that discuss the criticality of spiritual knowledge include John 8:31-32, 2 Peter 1:5-6, 2 Peter 3:17-18, Colossians 1:9-10, and Romans 10:1-3.

[375] Jeremiah 17:9 NASU

[376] Proverbs 28:26 NASU

[377] Ecclesiastes 11:9 NASU

.

CHAPTER 13

....

Childlike Faith

The word *childlike*[378] sometimes refers to a pleasant characteristic exhibited by an adult, but typical of children. Consider the following examples.

- As Layla watched the clowns entertain the audience, she laughed with childlike delight.

- Although a scientist for several years, Demos still gazes at the Milky Way with childlike wonder.

- Aravis cheered with childlike glee as her daughter accepted the award.

---

[378] *Childlike* vs. *childish* – No grammatical rule dictates when to utilize *childlike* versus *childish*. They function as exact synonyms.

At other times, we utilize *childlike* to describe a less-than-pleasing quality observed in a grown person, but common in a child.

- The lawyer's childlike voice continued to annoy the judge and jury.
- The women shunned the new club member who wore childlike clothing.
- The steel worker's childlike mannerisms alienated him from his peers.

Naivety,[379] an expected trait of children, renders them easily led astray. Lacking informed judgment, they tend to bypass truth, while favoring foolish myths, fairytales, and superstitions. Only study and experience can remedy their immaturity.

Likewise, Christians who have not matured *spiritually*, who linger in childlike faith, lack informed judgment. Deficient in their understanding of God's Scriptures, they remain susceptible to human theologies.[380] Only with study and experience can they overcome their spiritual immaturity.

During the first century A.D., some Christians did not develop normal spiritual growth, but lagged in immature faith. Reflect on the following passages in which Jesus' apostle Paul expressed disappointment in the Christians of Corinth due to their *childlike* faith.

---

[379] Naivety – a characteristic of someone who lacks knowledge and experience

[380] Theology, as referred to in this book, consists of any man-made system of interpretations, traditions, creeds, legends, myths, or combination of these items compiled or promoted by a religious leader, organization, denomination, or sect.

> *And I, brethren, **could not speak to you as to spiritual men**, but ... **as to infants** in Christ. I gave you milk to drink, not solid food; for you were not yet able to receive it. Indeed even now you are not yet able ....*[381]
>
> *Brethren, **do not be children in your thinking** ....* "[382]

God expressed disappointment in anyone who, after some time as a Christian, had not matured past that of a spiritual novice, beyond *childlike* faith. Consider how God, through one of His prophets, addressed those who had not increased their spiritual knowledge (substantiation) and trusting actions (conviction) over the course of their spiritual journey.

> *For though by this time you **ought to be teachers**, you have **need again for someone to teach you the elementary principles** of the oracles of God, and you have come to need milk and not solid food. For everyone **who partakes only of milk** ... is an **infant**. But **solid food is for the mature** ... Therefore leaving the elementary teaching ..., let us **press on to maturity** ....*[383]

God never urged anyone to maintain childlike faith,[384] a state of spiritual immaturity. Nonetheless, He *did* encourage Christians to assume *other* characteristics of young children, such as *humility*.

---

[381] 1 Corinthians 3:1-3 NASU (New American Standard Bible Update, 1995 revision). For more information about the NASU, see the copyright page, among the first pages of this book.)

[382] 1 Corinthians 14:20 NASU

[383] Hebrews 5:12-6:1 NASU

[384] God never used the term *childlike faith* in His Scriptures.

Humility

From time to time Jesus' apostles[385] fell short of His expectations. Had Jesus handpicked you or me to literally walk with Him on Earth for three years, we may have also found humility difficult to manage. Nevertheless, Jesus directed His apostles to assume humility, like that of a child. Note, though, He never encouraged His apostles to revert to childlike faith.

> *There arose ... a dispute among them* [Jesus' apostles][386] *as to which one of them was regarded to be greatest.*[387]

> *At that time, the disciples* [Jesus' apostles] *approached Jesus saying, "Who, then, is greater in the Kingdom of the Heavens?"*[388]

> *And having called over a small child, He stood him in the middle of them, and said, "I tell <u>you</u>[389] truly, unless <u>you</u> change <u>your</u> ways and become like the small children, <u>you</u> certainly will not enter into the Kingdom of the Heavens. Whoever, then, **humbles** himself as this small child, he is the greater person in the Kingdom of the Heavens.*[390]

---

[385] Apostle – *transliteration* of the Greek word *apóstolos* (ä-pŏ-stŏ-lŏs), ἀπόστολος, a common Greek word describing any delegate. When *transliterating*, a translator spells out an approximation of the original language's pronunciation of a word, using the alphabet of the second language. Within the Scriptures, "apostles" typically refers to the 12 followers chosen by Jesus to officially represent Him. For lists of the original twelve, see Matthew 10:1-4; Mark 3:13-19; Luke 6:12-16; and Acts 1:13 (which excludes Judas Iscariot, who had died).

[386] The author added [Jesus' apostles] to clarify the context.

[387] Luke 22:24 NASU

[388] Matthew 18:1 BT

[389] To convey the intent of the Greek text, the BT (Bagby Translation) marks *you* and *your* with a double underscore when plural (i.e., <u>you</u>, <u>your</u>).

[390] Matthew 18:2-4 BT; In this passage, Jesus spoke within the context of *humility*, not childlike faith. Furthermore, neither the preceding context, nor the subsequent context, concerns faith.

The apostles had failed to apply an earlier lesson they heard Jesus teach during a hillside chat.

> *Fortunate are the poor in spirit,*[391] *because the Kingdom of the Heavens is theirs.*[392]

Christian leaders continued to stress humility in the early church. For example, Paul compelled the Christians in the city of Philippi,

> *Do nothing from selfishness or empty conceit, but with* **humility** *of mind regard one another as more important than yourselves; do not merely look out for your own personal interests, but also for the interests of others.*[393]

Although Jesus never told His followers to regress into *childlike faith*, He did insist that they exercise humility, a trait common in small children.

---

[391] "Poor in spirit" served as an idiomatic expression meaning "humble" (Isaiah 66:1-2; 1 Peter 3:8-9). For more information regarding idiomatic expressions, see "Glossary."

[392] Matthew 5:3 BT

[393] Philippians 2:3-4 NASU; See also Ephesians 4:1-3; Colossians 3:12-13; James 1:21; 4:6,10; and 1 Peter 3:8-9; 5:5-7.

The Kingdom of the Heavens
Is of Such as These

Like us, Jesus' apostles sometimes had to hear a lesson more than once before they appreciated its meaning and applied it to their lives. Not long after Jesus had stood the small boy in their midst and explained His desire for them to demonstrate humility, the issue of spiritual attributes surfaced again.

> *Small children[394] were brought to Him so that He might lay His hands on them and pray, but the disciples scolded them.*
>
> *To the contrary, Jesus said, "Let the small children be and do not prevent them from coming to Me. For the Kingdom of the Heavens[395]* **is** *of such as these."[396]*

The Greek verb *estín* (ĕs-tǐn),[397] here translated "is," forms the third-person singular present active indicative grammatical construct of the infinitive[398] *eínai* (ĕí-näï),[399] which means "to be." Regardless, some translators incorrectly paraphrase Jesus' statement

---

[394] In Luke 18:15, Luke indicated that those small children included infants.

[395] New Testament writers utilized both "heaven" and "heavens" synonymously to communicate the same thing, making no distinction in meaning between the singular and plural forms of the word. To remain as closely parallel to the words originally penned as practical, the BT (Bagby Translation) employs the plural *heavens* each time a writer utilized the plural form of the word in the Greek text.

[396] Matthew 19:13-14 BT; See Mark 10:13-16 and Luke 18:15-17 for parallel passages.

[397] *Estín* (ĕs-tǐn), ἐστὶν

[398] Infinitive – a verb form with no indication of person, number, mood, or tense (Examples of infinitives include *to eat*, *to run*, and *to swim*.)

[399] *Eínai* (ĕí-näï), εἶναι

something similar to, "the Kingdom of the Heavens *belongs to*[400] such as these," instead of translating it precisely as Jesus explained, "*is* of such as these." Jesus indicated that, at the time He spoke to those disciples, the Kingdom of the Heavens consisted of beings who possessed traits similar to those of the children brought to Him ("*is* of such as these").

Jesus did not intend to convey that those residing in the Kingdom of the Heavens possess childlike, immature faith. Remember, His apostle Paul wrote to the Corinthian Christians,

*Brethren, **do not be children in your thinking** ....*[401]

Bear in mind, God defined faith as "the **substantiation** of things being hoped for, the **conviction** of things not seen."[402] One must *think maturely* to *substantiate* that for which one hopes.[403] Consequently, Paul instructed the Christians in Ephesus,

*We are **no longer to be children**, tossed here and there by waves and carried about by every wind of doctrine ... we are to **grow up** in all aspects into Him who is the head, even Christ ...."*[404]

Beware of anyone who urges you to aspire to *childlike faith*.

---

[400] Had Jesus said "belongs to," Matthew would have employed the present tense of the Greek infinitive *motóoho* (mŏ-tŏk-ō), μετέχω Instead, he used the present tense of the infinitive *eínai* (ĕĭ-năĭ), εἶναι, "to be."
[401] 1 Corinthians 14:20 NASU
[402] Hebrews 11:1 BT
[403] 1 Corinthians 13:11
[404] Ephesians 4:14-15 NASU

***

Contemplation Point

- In addition to humility, list a few spiritual traits[405] residents in the Kingdom of the Heavens (the spiritual realm) could have in common with human toddlers and infants.

---

[405] In this chapter, we rationally concluded God never directed anyone to maintain immature, childlike faith.

CHAPTER 14

....

Two Sure Ways to Increase Your Faith

Have you asked God to increase your faith, but noticed no apparent improvement? Sure, He has the *power* to saturate your brain with complete spiritual knowledge. Jesus promised such to His apostles.[406] In addition, He has the *capability* to fill anyone's spirit with total trust.[407] Yet, *never* has God given reason for us to expect Him to infuse *every* Christian with comprehensive knowledge, complete trust, or both.

---

[406] John 14:26; John 16:13 – The context of these two passages presents Jesus making promises *specifically* to His apostles, not to *all* Christians.

[407] 1 Corinthians 12:8-9; In verse 9, the Greek word *pístis* (pĭs-tĭs, πίστις), best translates as "trust," instead of "faith." Here, Paul addressed both factors of faith. In verse 8, he mentioned **knowledge** and in verse 9, he referred to **trust**. (NOTE: *Pístis* can translate as "trust," "belief," or "faith," depending on the context in which a writer used the word.)

God explained that He did not give every Christian the same capacities. Paul stressed that point as he asked the Corinthian believers,

> *All are not apostles, are they? All are not prophets, are they? All are not teachers, are they? All are not workers of miracles, are they? All do not have gifts of healings, do they? All do not speak with tongues, do they? All do not interpret do they?*[408]

Likewise, not everyone remains at an identical level of faith. God typically develops a Christian's faith[409] by providing opportunities to

1. Increase *knowledge* of His Scriptures and
2. Increase *trust* by applying that knowledge.

---

[408] 1 Corinthians 12:29-30 NASU

[409] Remember, **knowledge** (substantiated fact) **x trust** (conviction, trusting action, follow-through) = **faith**

Increase Your Knowledge (to Increase Faith)

As your faith ***grows***[410]
(Paul to the Corinthian Christians)

When Jesus asked His apostles, "Where is your faith?"[411] He held each of them accountable for the fitness of their faith. In addition, when Paul wrote "as your faith *grows*"[412] to the disciples in the city of Corinth, he expressed his expectation that they would increase their faith.

Peter, another of Jesus' apostles, urged the Christians of his day to cultivate faith by building their knowledge base, together with other dynamics of spiritual growth. He directed them,

> *Applying all diligence, in your **faith** supply moral excellence, and in your moral excellence, **knowledge**, and in your knowledge, self-control, and in your self-control, perseverance, and in your perseverance, godliness, and in your godliness, brotherly kindness, and in your brotherly kindness, love. For if these qualities are yours and are **increasing**, they render you neither useless nor unfruitful in the **true knowledge** of our Lord Jesus Christ. For he who lacks these qualities is **blind** ....*[413]

Furthermore, Paul encouraged his protégé evangelist Timothy to "pursue" faith,[414] reminding him that from childhood he had advanced his faith through that which he had "learned and become convinced of."[415] Timothy developed his faith by learning

---

[410] 2 Corinthians 10:15 NASU
[411] Luke 8:25 NASU
[412] 2 Corinthians 10:15 NASU
[413] 2 Peter 1:5-9 NASU
[414] 1 Timothy 6:11-12 NASU; 2 Timothy 2:22 NASU
[415] 2 Timothy 3:14-15 NASU

and then *substantiating* (becoming convinced of) the validity of what his teachers[416] had taught him.

Like Timothy and other Christians of the first century, you can increase your faith by expanding your knowledge of God's Scriptures.

> *Faith is the* **substantiation** *of things being hoped for,*
> *the* **conviction** *of things not seen.*
> (Hebrews 11:1 BT)

FAITH	=	KNOWLEDGE	×	TRUST
		(Substantiated Fact, Fact-based Belief)		(Conviction, Works of Faith, Trusting Action Based on Knowledge, Follow-through)

***

Contemplation Point

- How will you increase your *knowledge* of the Scriptures?

---

[416] 2 Timothy 1:5; 3:15

Increase Your Trust (to Increase Faith)

At one point, Jesus' apostles begged Him, "Increase our faith!"[417] A little reflection reveals that the answer to their petition rested within them. Although they increased their knowledge by watching Jesus and listening to His teachings, their weakness lay in failing to implement what they knew. They did not sufficiently *trust* that which they had come to know.

Remember the stories of faithful people you have read in the Scriptures. Count on God to fulfill His promises to those who remain faithful to Him. Consider the wholesome lifestyle you have discovered from His teachings. Trust that which you have come to know. Take action.

***

Contemplation Point

- How will you increase your *trust* in what you know about God and His promises?

---

[417] Luke 17:5 NASU

Increasing Faith: A Case Study

David, the Lions, the Bears, and Goliath

David's intense faith, his conviction to act on that which he had substantiated concerning God, moved the Creator to describe him as "a man after My heart, who will do all My will."[418] As you read the following story of the battle between the giant Goliath and David, note the knowledge David gained during previous battles with bears and lions. Observe how his past *substantiation* and *conviction* strengthened his faith, making him ready to fight Goliath. He *knew* and *trusted* God would give him victory.[419]

***

The Philistine[420] army again waged war against Israel. Camped on the west side of Elah Valley, 11 miles[421] southwest of Jerusalem, they waited.

Saul, king of Israel, arrived with his defense force and set up camp on the opposite side of the valley, about a half mile[422] from the Philistines.

David's three older brothers, warriors, stared across the valley with their comrades. Into the basin strutted a Philistine soldier over nine feet tall, clad with scaled bronze armor and a spear sturdy enough to sport an 18-pound iron spearhead.

---

[418] Acts 13:22 NASU; 1 Kings 11:4

[419] 1 Samuel 17:34-37

[420] Following Israel's conquest of the land God had long ago assured Abraham He would give to His descendants, the Philistines continued to control a small coastal region to the west of Jerusalem along the Mediterranean Sea. The Israelites called the land of the Philistines *Palásheth* (päl-å-shĕth), meaning "break through," in the sense of invaders. Philistia, an evil nation, proved a nemesis of Israel throughout most of its history.

[421] 18 kilometers

[422] 0.8 kilometer

Choose a man for yourselves and let him come down to me. If he is able to fight with me and kill me, then we will become your servants; but if I prevail against him and kill him, then you shall become our servants and serve us. ... I defy the ranks of Israel this day; give me a man that we may fight together.[423]

For 40 days, the two armies remained in their respective camps as Goliath made his way down to the valley floor each morning and evening to shout his challenge.

The 40th day, David's father gave him a break from tending the sheep and sent him to the front line to deliver a package of food to his brothers. He arrived that evening in time to watch the giant swagger into position below.

In terror, some of the soldiers asked David,

"Have you seen this man who is coming up? Surely he is coming up to defy Israel."[424]

Disappointed with their demeanor, David tried to embolden them, saying,

"Who is this uncircumcised Philistine, that he should taunt the armies of the living God?"[425]

Word spread quickly about this young man who seemed unafraid of Goliath. It did not take long for the news to reach the royal tent. King Saul, desperate after 40 days of Goliath's jeering, summoned David.

---

[423] 1 Samuel 17:8-10 NASU
[424] 1 Samuel 17:25 NASU
[425] 1 Samuel 17:26 NASU

> *David said to Saul, "Let no man's heart fail on account of him* [Goliath];*[426] your servant will go and fight with this Philistine.*
>
> *Then Saul said to David, "You are not able to go against this Philistine to fight with him; for you are but a youth[427] while he has been a warrior from his youth."*
>
> *But David said to Saul, "Your servant was tending his father's sheep. When a lion or a bear came and took a lamb from the flock, I went out after him and attacked him, and rescued it from his mouth; and when he rose up against me, I seized him by his beard and struck him and killed him.*
>
> *Your servant has killed both the lion and the bear; and this uncircumcised Philistine will be like one of them, since he has taunted the armies of the living God."*
>
> *And David said, "The Lord who delivered me from the paw of the lion and from the paw of the bear, He will deliver me from the hand of this Philistine."*
>
> *And Saul said to David, "Go, and may the Lord be with you."[428]*

Imagine yourself as energized by godly *substantiation* and *conviction* as David. Observing such faith, God would also describe you as a person "after My heart, who will do all My will."[429]

> *Faith is the **substantiation** of things being hoped for, the **conviction** of things not seen.*
> (Hebrews 11:1 BT)

---

[426] The author added [Goliath] to clarify the context.

[427] Saul's reference to David as a "youth" indicates David had not yet reached 20 years of age, the minimum required in Israel for a man to go to war (Numbers 1:3, 20-45).

[428] 1 Samuel 17:32-37 NASU

[429] Acts 13:22 NASU; 1 Kings 11:4

***

Contemplation Points

1. What gave David sufficient faith to go one-on-one against the giant, with absolute confidence of victory?

2. What would help you develop a faith like that of David's?

The Increase in David's Faith

David had developed the faith God described in Hebrews 11:1, the faith He desires us all to have. David would have scored well on the faith equation.

KNOWLEDGE	×	TRUST	=	FAITH
(Substantiated Fact, Fact-based Belief)		(Conviction, Trusting Action Based on Knowledge, Works of Faith, Follow-through)		(Knowledgeable, Trusting Action)

However, God did not pit David against Goliath while David possessed childlike faith. God first provided opportunities for David to build his faith while he served his family caring for sheep. David described part of the growth process of his faith to King Saul.

At times, a lion or bear would attack the flock and carry away a lamb. Having come to **know** God, David also **trusted** Him to help him fulfill his duty as a shepherd. As David told Saul, "I went out after him and attacked him, and rescued it from his mouth."[430] He counter-attacked the aggressor.

Neither lion nor bear welcomes interference with a meal. Consequently, the wild animal turned to confront the rescuer. Yet, David did not retreat. He assured King Saul that he "seized him by his beard and struck him and killed him."[431]

David did not say how many times he had faced down a bear or lion. He merely informed King Saul he did not shirk his responsibility. When necessary, he battled lions and bears, intruders who perceived no risk in snatching a lamb from a shepherd boy. David now found himself prepared to fight the giant who dared

---

[430] 1 Samuel 17:34-35 NASU
[431] 1 Samuel 17:35 NASU

"taunt the armies of the living God?"[432]

Each challenge further *substantiated* David's **knowledge** that God would help him. Each peril strengthened his *conviction* that God would not fail him. Each aggressor prepared David to **trust** the One he had come to **know** so well. As a result, his **faith increased**.

***

Contemplation Points

1. How has God provided you opportunities to develop your faith?

    a. What metaphorical[433] *lions* have you had to wrestle?

    b. With what metaphorical *bears* have you had to brawl?

2. Which factor of faith increased as a result of those opportunities?

    a. Knowledge (substantiation)? (If so, why?)

    b. Trust (conviction)? (If so, why?)

3. In which factor of faith do you need to grow more, knowledge (substantiation) or trust (conviction)?

    a. Explain how you became aware of your weaker factor of faith.

    b. How will you ensure your growth in that area?

---

[432] 1 Samuel 17:26 NASU

[433] A metaphor, a figure of speech, describes a characteristic or action of one noun (person, place, or thing) by replacing it in a sentence with a second *dissimilar* noun, suggesting a similarity between the two nouns. For more information about metaphors, see "Glossary."

CHAPTER 15

···

The Race Lying Before Us

Jesus' apostles pleaded with Him, "Increase our faith!"[434] You may have done the same. I have. However, in my ignorance, I did not anticipate the challenge of *bears* and *lions*.

Yet, that did not stop God from answering my request. He allowed the *wild beasts* to exercise my faith. Along the way, my knowledge of and trust in God increased to a level at which He could pit me against giants to come.

Nonetheless, I never enjoyed grappling with lions and bears. The joy came after the victory. Those victories belonged to the Lord.[435]

Even so, the ever-increasing faith belongs to me. It can also belong to you. Expand your knowledge of our Creator and deepen your trust in Him, then remain ready for the lions and bears.

---

[434] Luke 17:5 NASU
[435] 1 Samuel 17:46-47

> *Let us run with endurance the race lying before us,*
> *fixing our eyes on Jesus,*
> *the starter and finisher of the faith* [race].[436]
> (Hebrews 12:1-2 BT)

As you run the race of faith, recall the following passages through which God clarifies *His* perspective concerning your knowledge of Him and your trust in His dependability.

_____

[436] "The starter and finisher of the faith" translates precisely from the Greek text. The author added [race] to clarify the context.

Knowledge (God's Perspective)

I delight in loyalty rather than sacrifice,
*And in the **knowledge of God**[437] rather than burnt offerings.*[438]
(God to Israel)

***

*"So let us **know,** let us press on to **know the Lord**."*[439]
(God's prophet Hosea to Israel)

***

And this I pray,
that your love may abound still more and more
*in **real knowledge** and all discernment.*[440]
(Jesus' apostle Paul to the Philippians)

***

*Be **filled with the knowledge of His will***
in all spiritual wisdom and understanding,
so that you will walk in a manner worthy of the Lord,
to please Him in all respects, bearing fruit in every good work and
increasing in the knowledge of God.[441]
(Jesus' apostle Paul to the Colossians)

***

Grow in** the grace and **knowledge
of our Lord and Savior Jesus Christ.[442]
(Jesus' apostle Peter to the Christians of his day)

---

[437] For emphasis, the author has placed selected words in bold font within passages of Scripture quoted in this book.
[438] Hosea 6:6 NASU
[439] Hosea 6:3 NASU
[440] Philippians 1:9 NASU
[441] Colossians 1:9-10 NASU
[442] 2 Peter 3:18 NASU

Trust (God's Perspective)

*And those who **know** Your name
will put their **trust** in You.*[443]
(God's prophet David to God)

***

*Offer the sacrifices of righteousness,
And **trust** in the Lord.*[444]
(God's prophet David to his enemies)

***

*Put your **trust** in the Lord your God
and you will be established.*[445]
(King Jehoshaphat to the Judahites)

***

*Blessed is the man who **trusts** in the Lord
And whose **trust** is the Lord.*[446]
(God to the residents of Judah)

***

*So help us, O Lord our God,
for we **trust** in You.*[447]
(King Asa of Judah to God)

---

[443] Psalm 9:10 NASU
[444] Psalm 4:5 NASU
[445] 2 Chronicles 20:20 NASU
[446] Jeremiah 17:7 NASU
[447] 2 Chronicles 14:11 NASU

Faith (God's Perspective)

*"So then, all who **hear these words** [knowledge, substantiation][448]*
of Mine and
***do them** [trusting action, conviction][449]*
can be compared to a wise man who built his house on the bedrock.
Then the rain came down, and the flooded rivers came, and the
winds blew and beat upon that house. Yet it did not fall, because
it had been founded on the bedrock. "[450]
(Jesus to you and me)

***

For in this way God loved the world, insomuch that He gave His
*only born Son, that everyone **having faith in** Him might not perish,*
but might have eternal life.
(John 3:16 BT)

***

*But **without faith** it **is impossible to please Him**, for it is necessary*
*that the one coming to God **have faith** that He is and that He is a*
rewarder of those who seek Him out.
(Hebrews 11:6 BT)

***

*Faith is the **substantiation** of things being hoped for,*
*the **conviction** of things not seen.*
(Hebrews 11:1 BT)

---

[448] The author added [knowledge, substantiation] to clarify the significance of "hear these words."

[449] The author added [trusting actions, conviction] to clarify the significance of "do them."

[450] Matthew 7:24-25 BT; "Founded on the bedrock" = faith in Jesus (knowledge × trust)

Strengthen Your Faith

Increase Your Knowledge

God has provided you with His Scriptures to build your knowledge base. Come to know His story – *your* story. Read the Scriptures from cover to cover, again and again and again and again.

During the first reading, you may want to use a one-year reading schedule. Do that only once.

Afterward, read through slowly to understand what you read. Savor each story. Meditate on the lessons. You may require years to complete each future reading of the Book. That doesn't matter. You'll increase your knowledge, not merely read the words. Your faith will increase.

Increase Your Trust

When faced with trials, *remember*. Remember the stories you learned from God's Scriptures.

Remember Noah, Abraham, Isaac, Joseph, Moses, Deborah, Shadrach, Meshach, Abed-nego, Daniel, Jesus, Peter, James, John, Stephen, Paul, and all our other heroes of faith.

Remember David's clashes with the lions and bears that threatened the lives of his sheep. Remember how those skirmishes prepared him to face down Goliath. Wrestle your lions. Struggle with your bears. Get ready to battle your Goliaths.

Since we have so great a cloud of witnesses surrounding us,
let us also lay aside every encumbrance and
the sin which so easily entangles us, and
let us run with endurance the race that is set before us,
fixing our eyes on Jesus
(Hebrews 12:1-2 NASU)

Build your knowledge.

Exercise your trust.

STRENGTHEN YOUR FAITH!

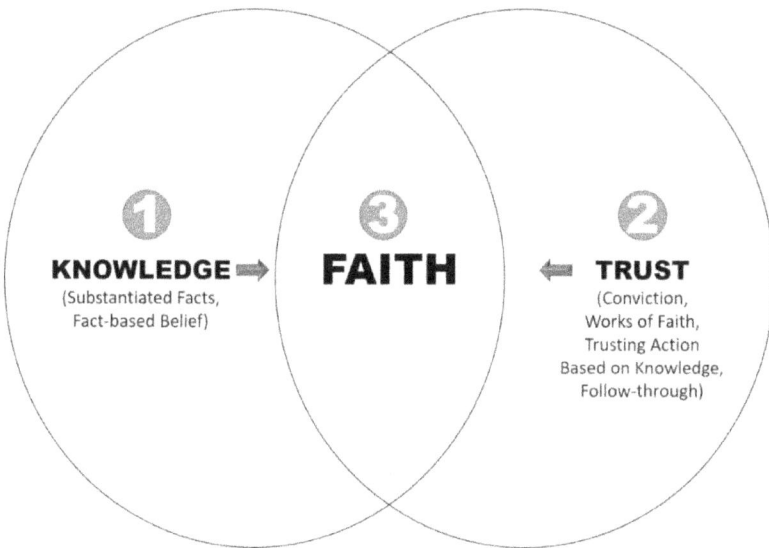

① **KNOWLEDGE** ➡ **FAITH** ⬅ **TRUST** **②**
(Substantiated Facts,   **③**   (Conviction,
Fact-based Belief)   Works of Faith,
                                           Trusting Action
                                  Based on Knowledge,
                                      Follow-through)

FAITH =	**KNOWLEDGE**	×	**TRUST**
	(Substantiated Fact, Fact-based Belief)		(Conviction, Trusting Action Based on Knowledge, Works of Faith, Follow-through)

Appendix 1: What About Grace?

This book addresses the two fundamental dynamics of faith, *knowledge* (substantiation) and *trust* (conviction). Perhaps a future writing will discuss in more detail how God's grace (unmerited benevolence) relates to faith.

For now, consider Paul's comments to Christians in the cities of Rome and Ephesus. He explained to them that faith serves as the conduit[451] through which a Christian enters God's grace.

To the Roman believers Paul wrote,

> *Having been justified by faith, we have peace with God through our Lord Jesus Christ, through whom also we have obtained our **introduction by faith into this grace** in which we stand; and we exult in hope of the glory of God.*[452]

---

[451] Conduit – a channel through which something can move
[452] Romans 5:1-2 NASU

To the disciples in Ephesus he added,

For ***by grace*** *you have been saved* ***through faith*** ....[453]

The *power* of saving faith resides in God's grace. He extends His saving grace to believers whose actions demonstrate their faith in Him. Only by His grace does a Christian's faith result in salvation.

Take to heart God's requirement that you activate your faith.

Faith without works [of faith][454] *is* ***useless***.[455]

***

As indeed the body without a spirit is dead,
so also, faith without works [of faith] *is* ***dead***.[456]

***

Not *all those who say to Me, 'Lord, Lord,'*
will enter the Kingdom of the Heavens, but rather
the one ***doing***[457] *the will of My Father*
who is in the Heavens.[458]
(Jesus to His Followers)

---

[453] Ephesians 2:8 NASU

[454] The author added [of faith] to clarify the context.

[455] James 2:20 BT; BT (Bagby Translation) designates a passage of Scripture translated by Dr. Chuck Bagby. For more information regarding the BT, see "Appendix 5: Bagby Translation (BT)."

[456] James 2:26 BT

[457] "Doing" corresponds to the second dynamic of faith presented in Hebrews 11:1, conviction (trusting action, follow-through).

[458] Matthew 7:21 BT

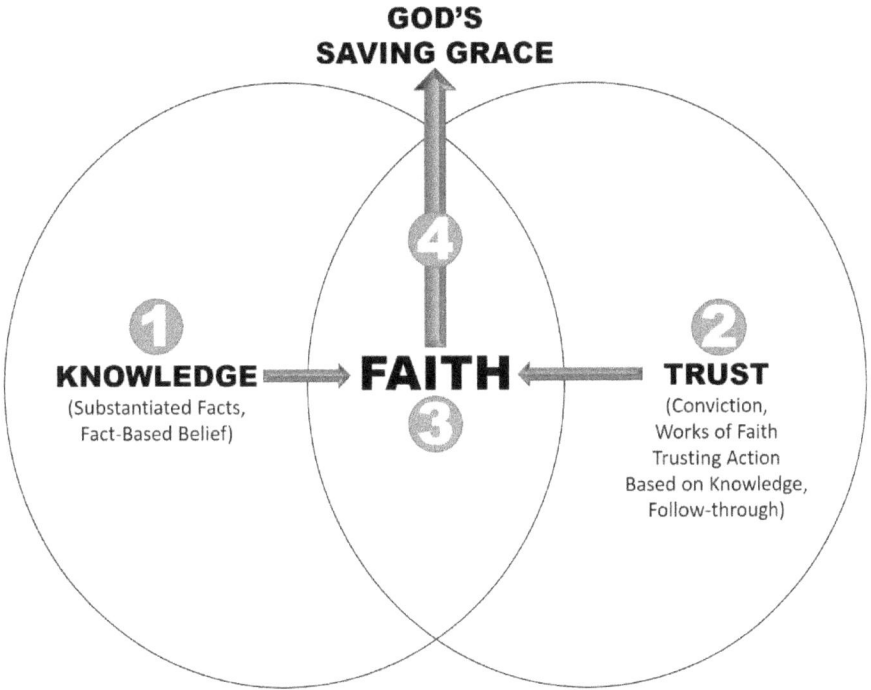

*For **by grace** you have been saved **through faith***[459]

---

[459] Ephesians 2:8 NASU

Appendix 2: What About the Holy Spirit?

Bear in mind that this book examines the two fundamental dynamics of faith, *knowledge* (substantiation) and *trust* (conviction). Perhaps a future writing will discuss in more detail how the Holy Spirit relates to a Christian's faith.

For now, reflect on Paul's statements to the Christians living in the region of Galatia, and others residing in the city of Thessalonica.

To the Galatian believers Paul wrote,

*For we **through the Spirit, by faith**,*
are waiting for the hope of righteousness.[460]

To the Thessalonian disciples he added,

*But we should always give thanks to God ... for **salvation** through **sanctification by the Spirit** and **faith** in the truth.*[461]

---

[460] Galatians 5:5 NASU
[461] 2 Thessalonians 2:13 NASU

Appendix 3: What About the Leap of Faith?

Mankind typically understands *a leap of faith* to have taken place when a person draws a conclusion based on subjective[462] feelings[463] rather than objective[464] reason. Søren Kierkegaard (1813-1855 A.D.), a Danish existentialist,[465] became a popular evangelist of the *leap* philosophy. Although Kierkegaard never used the term *a leap of faith*, he did apply the *leap* model to multiple contexts within his writings, including belief in the existence of God. Over time, popular religious culture transformed Kierkegaard's *leap* into the trendy figure of speech "a leap of faith." Any earlier clue to the origin of the *leap of faith* doctrine eludes discovery.

A search of the Scriptures, however, reveals that God's definition of faith requires substantiation, proof through objective analysis[466] – not a leap based on subjective feelings.

Faith is the **substantiation** *of things being hoped for,*
the conviction of things not seen.
(Hebrews 11:1 BT)

---

[462] Subjective – based on feelings rather than logic
[463] See "Chapter 12 – Deceitful or Truthful Feelings?"
[464] Objective – based on logic rather than feelings
[465] Existentialism proclaims no one can possess a definite knowledge of right, wrong, good, evil, moral, or immoral, etc.
[466] See "Chapter 3 – Faith Defined by God."

The Christians in Rome faced intense social pressure from the existentialist types of their era to compromise their faith, to deny the reality of one true God. The apostle Paul explained to those believers that objective analysis of the vast circumstantial evidence of "what has been made"[467] indicates intelligent design – patterns that point to the Designer-Maker. He wrote to the Roman believers,

> *That which is known about God is evident within them; for God made it evident to them. For since the creation of the world His invisible attributes, His eternal power and divine nature, have been clearly seen, being* **understood through what has been made***, so that they are without excuse.*[468]

You, too, should objectively consider "what has been made." Employ the critical-thinking[469] ability God gave you. Consider the circumstantial evidence. Analyze the patterns of functional design in the universe. Substantiate the reality of your Designer-Maker.

---

[467] Romans 1:20 NASU; See also Psalm 19:1-2

[468] Romans 1:19-20 NASU

[469] For a discussion of critical thinking, see "Chapter 3 – Faith Defined by God," heading "Faith (*Pístis*)," subheading "Critical Thinking."

Appendix 4: The Non-Functional
Additive Equation

At first reading, the two essential factors of faith God sets forth in Hebrews 11:1, substantiation (knowledge) and conviction (trust), appear to share an additive[470] relationship. However, the results of the following Practical Application Test prove the *additive* faith equation unworkable.

*Faith is the **substantiation** of things being hoped for,*
*the **conviction** of things not seen.*
(Hebrews 11:1 BT)

FAITH ≠	KNOWLEDGE	+	TRUST
	(Substantiated Fact)		(Conviction, Trusting Action Based on Knowledge)

---

[470] Additive – relating to the operation of mathematical addition

Practical Application Test (Additive Equation)

Suppose a person learns and substantiates half of what God has made possible to know through study of His Scriptures. The *knowledge addend*[471] within the equation would amount to 50%. Likewise, if four out of five times an opportunity occurs, that person confidently acts on the 50% he knows, the *trust addend* equals 80% (i.e., $4 \div 5 = .80 = 80\%$). Using the additive equation, the calculation of 50% knowledge plus 80% trust would total 130% faith.

$$.50 \text{ knowledge} + .80 \text{ trust} = 1.30 = 130\% \text{ faith}$$

The additive equation calculates that this individual would have achieved greater than 100% faith, an unattainable, irrational outcome.

50%	**+**	**80%**	**=**	**130%**
KNOWLEDGE		**TRUST**		**FAITH**
(Substantiated Fact)		(Conviction, Trusting Action Based on Knowledge)		(Knowledgeable, Trusting Action)

The fact that no one can possess greater than 100% of anything proves the additive equation invalid.

---

[471] Addend – one of any number within a mathematical operation intended for addition to another number (e.g., within the calculation 50 + 80 = 130, the numbers 50 and 80 function as addends).

Appendix 5: Bagby Translation (BT)

Original Translation

The Bagby Translation (BT), an original work designed by Dr. Chuck Bagby for oral reading, demonstrates exceptional faithfulness to the Greek and Hebrew texts. When read aloud, as though telling the story in person, the BT virtually places the reader at the feet of God's prophets.

The BT does not attempt a word-for-word translation of the Greek or Hebrew, because the syntax,[472] idiomatic expressions,[473] and interjections[474] of the original language differ from ours. Rigid adherence to Greek or Hebrew syntax frequently produces

---

[472] Syntax – the orderly system by which words form clauses, phrases, and sentences

[473] Idiomatic expression – a figure of speech whose true significance one cannot understand by accepting the literal meaning of the individual words it contains (For further clarification, see "Idiomatic Expression" in "Glossary.")

[474] Interjection – a word or phrase used to exclaim, protest, or command (For illustrations, see "Interjection" in "Glossary.")

unintelligible sentences in English. Furthermore, a word-for-word translation of idiomatic expressions often communicates a meaning the writer never intended. Instead of translating word for word, the BT typically conveys the literal intent of the writer by replacing idiomatic expressions with their intended meanings, while placing the word-for-word translation in a footnote. The BT also employs English syntax and contextually-equivalent English interjections in its translation.

"Behold" in the Bagby Translation of Greek

Biblical writers, as well as the characters within their stories, use the Greek word *idoú* (ĭd-ŏú́)[475] as an interjection[476] at critical moments of a story to draw attention to a specific item or event. *Idoú* means "look."

Some translators continuously render *idoú* as "behold," which frequently produces awkward sentences in English. Others translate *idoú* as "lo," an archaic word. Still others omit *idoú* entirely from their translation, finding it difficult to fit the word smoothly into English. None of those methods effectively expresses the varied emphasis suggested by the diverse contexts[477] in which biblical authors apply the interjection.

English has many interjections from which to choose when one desires to grasp the attention of a reader or listener. Therefore, the BT renders *idoú* in various ways to complement the variety of contexts within which biblical writers employed the word. The list below contains interjections used in the BT to express the significance of *idoú* in its many contexts.

- Look
- Look here
- Look now
- See
- Observe

- Get this
- Pay attention
- Take note
- Listen

- Listen carefully
- Listen closely
- Listen now
- Listen to this

- Listen up
- Now listen
- Now listen carefully
- Now listen to this

---

[475] *Idoú* (ĭd-ŏú́), ἰδού

[476] Interjection – a word or phrase used to exclaim, protest, or command (For illustrations, see "Interjection" in "Glossary.")

[477] Context, the communication before and after a word or passage, often sheds light on the meaning intended by the writer or speaker.

Kingdom of the Heavens

New Testament writers utilized both *heaven* and *heavens* synonymously to communicate the same thing. To remain as closely parallel to the words of the original language text as practical, the Bagby Translation (BT) employs the plural *heavens* each time a biblical writer has utilized the plural form of the word (e.g., Matthew 3:2,16-17; 4:17; 5:3,10-11,16,19-20; Mark 1:10-11, John 1:51, 2 Corinthians 5:1, Ephesians 1:10, Acts 7:56; and others).

Bold Font

The BT occasionally highlights words in bold font. Although the highlights do not exist in the original language text, they help the reader follow the logical thought of passages.

You and Your

Readers of English frequently have difficulty determining whether a biblical writer employed the singular or plural of *you* and *your*. To convey the intent of the original language text, the BT marks *you* and *your* with a double underscore when plural (i.e., you, your).

Church Speak

Church speak, ambiguous vocabulary typically confined to *traditional* Christian religious discussion, tends to blur the exact meanings intended by biblical authors in their Greek and Hebrew texts and often leads Bible readers to misunderstand God's Scriptures. The BT avoids church speak by utilizing precise translations. The chart below presents a few examples of vocabulary employed by the BT in lieu of church speak.

CHURCH SPEAK	BAGBY TRANSLATION	PASSAGE
Baptize	Immerse	Matthew 3:11
Blessed	Fortunate Privileged	Matthew 5:3 Matthew 16:17
Confessing	Acknowledging	Matthew 3:6
Gospel	Good message Good news	Matthew 4:23 Matthew 11:5
Miracles	Supernatural acts	Matthew 7:22
Miraculous powers	Supernatural powers	Matthew 13:54
Preaching	Proclaiming	Matthew 3:1

Glossary

Apostle

A *transliteration* of the Greek word *apóstolos* (ä-pŏ-stŏ-lŏs), ἀπόστολος, a common Greek word describing any delegate. When *transliterating*, a translator spells out an approximation of the original language's pronunciation of a word using the alphabet of the second language. Within the Scriptures, "apostles" typically refers to the 12 followers chosen by Jesus to represent Him. For lists of the original twelve, see Matthew 10:1-4; Mark 3:13-19; Luke 6:12-16; and Acts 1:13 (which excludes Judas Iscariot, who had died).

Centurion

A centurion, a Roman army official, commanded around 100 soldiers in earlier times, but around 80 during Jesus' lifetime on Earth.

Church Speak

See "Appendix 5: Bagby Translation (BT)," heading "Church Speak."

Circumstantial Evidence

Circumstantial (indirect) evidence consists of proof, other than eye-witness confirmation, through which one can logically substantiate the existence of a fact. Just as the pattern of a fingerprint on glass *proves* a specific person touched that object, so also, design within the

183

universe, from the smallest subatomic particle to vast galaxies, establish the existence of an intelligent Designer-Creator.

Critical Thinking

Critical thinking occurs when one bases beliefs and behavior on the exercise of careful reasoning founded on sound evidence and intellectual integrity.

Context

Context, the communication positioned before and after a word or passage, often sheds light on the meaning intended by a writer or speaker.

Idiomatic Expression (Idiom)

An idiomatic expression, a figure of speech sometimes referred to as an "idiom," conveys a meaning impossible to understand by considering the literal sense of the individual words it contains. For example, the idiomatic expression in the sentence, "He is *pulling your leg*," expresses the same message as the more ordinary sentence, "He is *joking with you.*"

Indirect Evidence

See *circumstantial evidence*.

Infinitive

A verb form with no indication of person, number, mood, or tense (Examples of infinitives include to eat, to run, and to swim.)

Intellectual Integrity

To maintain intellectual integrity, one must remain 1) objective, 2) unslanted by preconceptions or biases, 3) free of contradictory beliefs, and 4) without self-deception.

Interjection   An interjection, a word or phrase used to exclaim, protest, or command, may express an emotion or a reaction and may draw attention to a specific item or event. An interjection can stand alone as a part of speech (e.g., Well!; Wow!; Look!; Hey!; Oh!; No!; Listen!).

Josephus   Titus Flavius Josephus, a Jewish general and historian, lived 37-100 A.D. He led the Judean defense when, in 66 A.D., the Roman army invaded Judea to suppress a widespread Jewish revolt. Although the Judean revolt failed, Josephus survived. He later lived in Rome, where he compiled his historical records.

Justify   To justify means to treat as not guilty. When God has "justified" someone, through His mercy and grace He regards that person as "just" (i.e., innocent of wrongdoings) despite past misconduct, because Jesus paid the penalty through His sacrificial crucifixion. Only the compelling blood of an innocent man's voluntary self-sacrifice could bridge the chasm separating a guilty human from God's favor (Hebrews 9:22; Leviticus 17:11).

Leap of Faith   See "Appendix 3: What About the Leap of Faith?"

Metaphor   Metaphor, a figure of speech, describes a characteristic or action of one noun (person, place, or thing) by comparing it with a second *dissimilar* noun to suggest a similarity between the two nouns. For example, the metaphor in the statement, "The truck maneuvered up the mountain on the winding *snake*," conveys the same message as the more ordinary sentence, "The truck maneuvered up the mountain on the winding *road*."

Oxymoron   Oxymoron, a two-word phrase containing terms defined by contradictory meanings, includes such confused verbiages as *cruel kindness*, *deafening silence*, *exact estimate*, *genuine imitation*, and *blind faith*. Although usually a two-word phrase, an oxymoron sometimes consists of two contradictory phrases.

Parallelism
Many languages employ parallelism, including the original languages in which God's prophets wrote His Scriptures. Parallelism, a literary rhetorical construct, occurs in prose, but more often in poetry (e.g., Psalms, Proverbs, etc.). The parallel structure balances ideas of equal importance, but the elements balanced do not always have identical meanings. Readers encounter numerous variations of the following six types of parallelism within the Scriptures.

1. **Synonymous** – the second concept remains synonymous with the first (Common in English)

   - The paddleboat steamed up Ole Man River, the muddy Mississippi.

   - "The heavens are telling of the glory of God; and their expanse is declaring the work of His hands." (Psalm 19:1 NASU)

2. **Synthetic** – builds on the first

   - "Faith is the substantiation of things being hoped for, the conviction of things not seen." (Hebrews 11:1 BT)

3. **Antithetic** – contrasts with the first

   - "My flesh and my heart may fail, but God is the strength of my heart and my portion forever." (Psalm 73:26 NASU)

4. **Climactic** – successive lines or phrases build to a climax and/or summary (as in Habakkuk 3:17-19 below)

- Builds

  - ➢ "Though the fig tree should not blossom and there be no fruit on the vines, though the yield of the olive should fail and the fields produce no food, though the flock should be cut off from the fold and there be no cattle in the stalls," (Habakkuk 3:17 NASU)

- Climax/summary

  - ➢ "Yet I will exult in the Lord, I will rejoice in the God of my salvation." (Habakkuk 3:18 NASU)

  - ➢ "The Lord God is my strength, and He has made my feet like hinds' feet, and makes me walk on my high places." (Habakkuk 3:19 NASU)

5. **Emphatic** – series of synonymous words or phrases used for emphasis

    - "You shall love the Lord your God with all your heart and with all your soul and with all your might."[478] (Deuteronomy 6:5 NASU)

6. **Eclectic** – interweaves different types of parallelism (as in Habakkuk 1:2-4 below)

    - Antithetic

        - "How long, O Lord, will I call for help, And You will not hear?" (Habakkuk 1:2a NASU)

        - "I cry out to You, 'Violence!' Yet You do not save." (Habakkuk 1:2b NASU)

    - Synonymous

        - "Why do You make me see iniquity, and cause me to look on wickedness?" (Habakkuk 1:3a NASU)

        - "Yes, destruction and violence are before me; Strife exists and contention arises."

---

[478] In Deuteronomy 6:5, through relatively synonymous phrases, the writer emphasizes entire dedication to God.

(Habakkuk 1:3b
NASU)

- Synthetic
  - ➢ "Therefore the law is
    ignored and justice is
    never upheld."
    (Habakkuk 1:4a
    NASU)
  - ➢ "For the wicked
    surround the
    righteous; therefore
    justice comes out
    perverted."
    (Habakkuk 1:4b
    NASU)

Pharisee   The Greek word rendered "Pharisee" is
Pharisaíos (făr-ĭs-äí-ŏs),[479] a Greek
transliteration of the Hebrew word *pharósh*
(făr-ŏsh),[480] which means "one who is
separated." Pharisees endeavored to separate
themselves from spiritual impurities. Their
sect consisted primarily of scholars, scribes,
and nonprofessionals from the lower economic
middle class. During Jesus' time on Earth they
numbered about 6,000. (Josephus, 1977, p.
358)[481] A number of priests allied with the
Pharisees,[482] although most aligned with the
Sadducees,[483] and some priests affiliated with
no sect.

---

[479] *Pharisaíos* (făr-ĭs-äí-ŏs), Φαρισαῖος

[480] *Pharósh* (făr-ŏsh), פרושׁ

[481] *The Antiquities of the Jews*, Book 17, Chapter 2, Paragraph 4; Titus
Flavius Josephus (jō-sĕ́-fəs), a Jewish general and historian, lived 37-
100 A.D. For more information regarding Josephus, see "Glossary."

[482] John 1:19,24; For more information concerning the Pharisee sect see the
book *Born to Die* (by Chuck Bagby), "Chapter 9 – Poisonous Snakes:
Pharisees & Sadducees," heading "Who Were the Pharisees? (Matthew
3:7)."

[483] For information concerning the Sadducee sect, see "Glossary." For more
information, see the book *Born to Die* (by Chuck Bagby), "Chapter 9 –
Poisonous Snakes: Pharisees & Sadducees," heading "Who Were the
Sadducees? (Matthew 3:7)."

Sadducee	The Greek word rendered "Sadducee" is *Saddoukaíos* (säd-dŏŭ-kä-ĭ́-ŏs).[484] The first part of the word, *Saddouk*, is a Greek transliteration of the Hebrew word *tsadák* (tsä-dǎk),[485] which means "to be right." Hence, a Sadducee viewed himself as a *righteous one.* Although their sect numbered less than the Pharisees, the Sadducees controlled all Temple activities in Jerusalem, basing their religious authority on social position and family lineage. Most priests allied with the Sadducees,[486] although a number of priests aligned with the Pharisees,[487] and some priests affiliated with no sect.
	For more information regarding the Sadducees, see the book *Born to Die* (by Chuck Bagby), "Chapter 9 – Poisonous Snakes: Pharisees & Sadducees," heading "Who Were the Sadducees? (Matthew 3:7)."

---

[484] *Saddoukaíos* (säd-dŏŭ-kä-ĭ́-ŏs), Σαδδουκαῖος

[485] *Tsadák* (tsä-dǎk), צדק

[486] For more information concerning the Sadducee sect, see the book *Born to Die* (by Chuck Bagby), "Chapter 9 – Poisonous Snakes: Pharisees & Sadducees," heading "Who Were the Sadducees? (Matthew 3:7)."

[487] John 1:19,24; For information concerning the Pharisee sect, see "Glossary." For more information, see the book *Born to Die* (by Chuck Bagby), "Chapter 9 – Poisonous Snakes: Pharisees & Sadducees," heading "Who Were the Pharisees? (Matthew 3:7)."

Scribes   The responsibilities of scribes evolved over ages. Prior to the Babylonian deportation,[488] a scribe served as an officer in the king's court who documented legal statutes.

A different type of scribe emerged around 458 B.C., upon the return of the first Judahites to Judea from the Babylonian deportation. At that time, a priest named Ezra "set his heart to study the law of the Lord and to practice it, and to teach His statutes and ordinances."[489] He became "a scribe skilled in the Law of Moses, which the Lord God of Israel had given."[490]

Following Ezra's lead, others joined him in scribal endeavors. They meticulously produced copies of the Scriptures and taught the Word of God to their countrymen. Those godly scribes chose not to document their personal teachings,[491] fearing others might come to consider their remarks equal in authority to God's Scriptures. Hence, one generation passed down their lessons orally to the next generation. Simon the Just, the last of that company of scribes, died around 290 B.C.,

---

[488] For more information about the deportation of Israelites to Babylonia, see the book *Born to Die* (by Chuck Bagby), "Chapter 2 – Kings & Scoundrels: Jesus' Ancestors," heading "The Babylonian Deportation (Matthew 1:11)."

[489] Ezra 7:10 NASU

[490] Ezra 7:6 NASU

[491] Ezra, the only known priest of God among the scribes of his era (Nehemiah 8:2,9;12:26), also served as one of God's prophets and wrote the biblical book (Ezra) to convey a message God delivered through him, not to communicate his personal remarks (2 Peter 1:20-21).

close to 180 years after Ezra began his work.

In 140 B.C., about 150 years after the death of Simon the Just, a new breed of scribes surfaced. Although they began with righteous motives, they deemed it necessary to document the verbal instruction of the scribes who came before them, desiring to preserve the *traditional* teachings for posterity.

Regrettably, over the decades that followed, that new community of scribes compelled everyone to adhere to the traditional teachings of the ancient scribes. Some scribes aligned with the chief priests[492] who led the Sadducee sect,[493] while others allied with the Pharisees.[494] The Pharisaic scribes came to teach that the "traditions of the elders" *superseded* the authority of the Scriptures.[495]

Jesus strongly condemned the practice of those

---

[492] Matthew 2:4; Luke 22:2,66; Matthew 16:21; 20:18; 21:15; 26:57; 27:41; Mark 8:31; 11:18,27; 14:1,43,53; 15:1,31; Luke 9:22; 19:47; 20:1,19; 23:10; Acts 4:5-6

[493] For more information concerning the Sadducee sect, see the book *Born to Die* (by Chuck Bagby), "Chapter 9 – Poisonous Snakes: Pharisees & Sadducees," heading "Who Were the Sadducees? (Matthew 3:7)."

[494] Mark 2:16; Luke 5:30; Acts 23:9; Matthew 5:20; 12:38; 15:1; 23:2,13-15,23,25,27,29; Mark 7:5; Luke 5:21; 6:7; 11:53; 15:2; John 8:3; For more information concerning the Pharisee sect, see the book *Born to Die* (by Chuck Bagby), "Chapter 9 – Poisonous Snakes: Pharisees & Sadducees," heading "Who Were the Pharisees? (Matthew 3:7)."

[495] Matthew 15:2-3,6

scribes[496] of Herod's day.[497]

For more information regarding scribes, see the book *Born to Die* (by Chuck Bagby), "Chapter 4 – The Magi Meet Herod, King of Judea," heading "Who Were the Scribes? (Matthew 2:4)."

Syntax   Syntax refers to the orderly system by which words form clauses, phrases, and sentences.

Theology   Theology, as referred to in this book, consists of any man-made system of interpretations, traditions, creeds, legends, myths, or combination of these items compiled or promoted by a religious leader, sect, denomination, or organization.

Transliterate   When transliterating, instead of translating a word, a translator *spells out* an approximation of the original language's *pronunciation* of the word using the alphabet of the second language. Translators often transliterate names and words that have no corresponding term in the second language. A transliteration, having no inherent meaning of its own, derives its meaning directly from the definition of the word in the original language.

If the second language contains a term carrying the same meaning as the word from

---

[496] Scribes – also referred to as *lawyers*, in relation to the Law of Moses and the traditions of the elders (Matthew 22:35; Luke 7:30; 10:25; 11:45-46,52; 14:3)

[497] Mark 12:38-40; Luke 20:46-47

the original language, no justification exists for the use of a transliteration. In that case, intellectual integrity mandates the translator employ a translation.

Pronunciation Symbols

SYMBOL	PRONUNCIATION
ā	"a" as in "ate"
ă	"a" as in "apple"
â	"a" as in "parent"
ä	"a" as in "palm"
ə	"a" as in "diagram"
b	"b" as in "bank"
d	"d" as in "dance"
ē	"e" as in "eel" "i" as in "police"
ĕ	"e" as in "let"
f	"f" as in "fat" "ph" as in "phantom"
g	"g" as in "got"
h	"h" as in "harmony"
ī	"i" as in "bite"
ĭ	"i" as in "bit" "y" as in "abyss"
k	"k" as in "kiss"
kh	"ch" as in "chorus"
l	"l" as in "lead"
m	"m" as in "many"

SYMBOL	PRONUNCIATION
n	"n" as in "not"
ngg	"ng" as in "angle"
ō	"o" as in "tote"
ŏ	"o" as in "obstruct"
ô	"aw" as in "awkward"
p	"p" as in "pit"
r	"r" as in "ran"
s	"s" as in "slick"
sh	"sh" as in "shop"
t	"t" as in "tin"
th	"th" as in "worth"
ū	"u" as in "fume"
ŭ	"u" as in "pup"
ü	"u" as in "crude" "oo" as in "toot"
û	"u" as in "turn"
y	"y" as in "yellow"
z	"z" as in "haze"

13-Week Class Schedule

Week **1** – Read "Preface" through the end of page 13.

Week **2** – Read page 15 through the end of page 27a.

Week **3** – Read page 27 through page 43.

Week **4** – Read page 45 through the end of page 61.

Week **5** – Read page 63 through page 72.

Week **6** – Read page 73 through the end of page 87.

Week **7** – Read page 89 through the end of page 104.

Week **8** – Read page 105 through the end of page 113.

Week **9** – Read page 115 through the end of page 123.

Week 10 – Read page 125 through the end of page 137.

Week 11 – Read page 139 through the end of page 145.

Week 12 – Read page 147 through the end of page 157.

Week 13 – Read page 159 through the end of page 176

References

Edersheim, A. (1874). *The Temple: Its Ministry and Service, as They Were at the Time of Jesus Christ.* London, England, United Kingdom: The Religious Tract Society.

Edersheim, A. (1881). *Sketches of Jewish Social Life in the Days of Christ.* New York, NY, USA: James Pott & Co.

Josephus, F. (1977). *The Complete Works of Flavius Josephus* (Fourteenth Printing ed.). (W. Whiston, Trans.) Grand Rapids, MI, USA: Kregel Publications.

About the Author

Evangelist

Chuck Bagby worked fulltime as an evangelist for ten years, completing foreign assignments in both Honduras and Argentina. Following that, while dedicating two decades to the business world, he continued to "do the work of an evangelist" (2 Timothy 4:5 NASU). He teaches today through *Burning Heart Bible Studies* seminars and books (www.BurningHeartBibleStudies.com).

Current Work

Chuck serves as a Consulting Professor of Biblical Studies for Nations University. Together with this, he conducts *The Jesus Story: What I Wish I Had Known* seminars. He also offers church leaders coaching in the implementation of his unique **T-E-A-M** leadership methodology.

Education

Chuck holds a PhD in biblical studies from the Theological University of America (TUA), having previously graduated from the Sunset International Bible Institute (SIBI). The University of Texas at San Antonio (UTSA) awarded him an MBA in International Business, with concentrations in international marketing and international finance. He earned a BA in Spanish Literature from the University of Missouri – Columbia.

Past Work

A former international business executive, Chuck specialized in team leadership, cross-cultural communication, and organizational turnarounds. Employing his unique **T-E-A-M** leadership methodology, he consistently transformed underperforming organizations into high-performance teams. He served on the Advisory Council of the College of Business at UTSA and on the Entrepreneurs' Roundtable at the same university. He has carried out business in Argentina, Bolivia, Canada, Chile, Colombia, El Salvador, England, Honduras, Mexico, Peru, Spain, Sweden, and Uruguay.

Special Request

Please let Chuck know something about you.

Send an e-mail to

AllForJesus@BurningHeartBibleStudies.com

www.BurningHeartBibleStudies.com

www.ingramcontent.com/pod-product-compliance
Lightning Source LLC
Chambersburg PA
CBHW060012050426
42448CB00012B/2719